Sue Schoenbeck has brought to light a mystery that each of us has struggled with in our own way. She has done this in layperson's terms, not in medical or psychological terminology. She has given all of us who work with and support the dying and their families, a very warm and loving understanding of this most feared transition of life as we know it now, to a life beyond our present earthly and physical life. Death does not have to be feared—it can be and should be a peaceful and rewarding experience.

Sue relates stories and experiences that can help us in a very peaceful and most gracious way move into a new existence, if we allow it to happen. Sue shares with us all the beautiful and fulfilling gift of presence that she has found with all people who have experienced the power and spirit of the Almighty, moving them through the final phases of their lives toward "The Final Entrance" to a new and beautiful existence beyond our imagination. It is something to work toward, to live for, with an enthusiasm and attitude that this life is indeed special, and is the stepping stone into something even greater and more fullfilling than what we have here.

—*Father Larry Heitke, Chaplain,William S. Middleton*
Veterans Memorial Hospital and St. Benedict's Center,
Madison, Wisconsin.

Sue Schoenbeck's story-style of presenting the material is refreshing and I think it is the best way to present the topic of near-death experiences (NDE). After all, the stories that people have from their NDEs are the proof that they exist and makes the whole phenomenon of NDEs more credible than a clinical, scientific approach as to how and why they occur. This book makes the subject matter of NDEs more approachable and less "spooky."

—*Reverend John D. Emmart, Director, Department of Pastoral Care, University of Wisconsin Hospital and Clinics.*

The Final Entrance

The Final Entrance

Journeys beyond Life

Susan L. Schoenbeck

PRAIRIE OAK PRESS
Madison, Wisconsin

Prairie Oak Press
821 Prospect Place
Madison, WI 53703

Typeset by KC Graphics, Madison, Wisconsin

Printed in the United States of America by BookCrafters, Chelsea, Michigan

Library of Congress Cataloging-in-Publication Data

Schoenbeck, Susan L.
    The Final Entrance: Journeys beyond life / Susan L. Schoenbeck.
        p.   cm.
    Includes bibliographical references.
    ISBN 1-879483-36-X (alk. paper)
    1. Near-death experiences   I. Title.
BF1045.N4S395   1997
133.9'01'3--dc21   97-1304
                                                              CIP

To my parents, Alvin and Marjorie Schoenbeck,
who gave me love,
and
the belief that there is more to life
than one's physical self.

For Jason, Max and Molly.
May Love and Light within all creation guide you.

Contents

Foreword

Sue Schoenbeck has written a remarkable book and has given it a remarkable title, at once both revealing and misleading. *Final Entrance* takes its meaning from the age-old metaphor, best known to us through Shakespeare's *As You Like It,* that "all the world's a stage." Schoenbeck dares us to think of dying not as an actor's exit at the play's finale, but as another entrance, perhaps for a final act not for public viewing.

This is a jarring thought for many of us, a contradictory thought, a strange and unnatural thought. And that's why I say Schoenbeck's title is also misleading: because there is nothing strange or unnatural about the stories in this book. In fact, her message is in part that dying is the most natural thing we do, and that these stories sound strange only to the extent that we try so hard to avoid them.

Who is Sue Schoenbeck to tell us this? She is first and foremost a compassionate person with a deep respect for folks struggling with their own "final entrances" and with those of their loved ones. Schoenbeck has worked in settings as diverse as an open heart surgical intensive care unit, a coronary care unit, a convalescent home, a nursing school, a university clinical science center, and a retirement community. She is not only a seasoned clinician and an accomplished teacher, but has also won awards for translating medical information into language meaningful and comprehensible to patients and their families. Her years of experience as a nurse, educator, researcher, and public speaker have brought her a variety of stories of people who have had brushes with death.

We are all too familiar with death as a physical process. Schoenbeck reminds us here that it is also a spiritual process, largely overlooked by caregivers because that aspect is not easily measured or described. Though she has taught in nursing schools and written articles for nursing journals, the wisdom in these pages is not the kind that can be found in medical texts. Nor is it the kind of wisdom dispensed by our religious traditions or by the "books of the dead" that have survived the ages. There is certainly a lot to be gleaned from both those sources, but what Schoenbeck offers us here is something quite different. It is the wisdom of her patients, of the folks who are able to share their experience of the transition from this world, usually without any inkling at all that they are spouting wisom.

Schoenbeck shares with us these accounts she has collected over the years, of profound death-related experiences such as visits from the spirits of deceased relatives, deathbed conversations with deceased loved ones, accurate premonitions of death, out-of-body experiences and otherworldly visions, and patients' struggles with the decision about whether to be resuscitated—and with how to tell family members about that decision. The thread that holds this tapestry together is Schoenbeck's respect for these folks and for their experiences. I am not talking about a polite clinical nod to the inescapable reality of these events, but rather an honest validation of the importance of human experience with the dying process.

For many readers, these stories may be a confirmation of their own experiences. For clinicians and scientists, Schoenbeck also includes a simple test of knowledge about near-death experiences and a brief description of her scholarly study of near-death experiences among people receiving cardiopulmonary resuscitation.

But stories and knowledge are not what this book is about; they are merely its vehicles. In a world of healthcare technology, this is a book about compassion. In a society proud of our medical conquests, this is a book about humility. In a culture impatient with "useless" experiences—and people—this is a book about respect.

We avoid dying people because we ourselves want to live and, because of that desire, try to stay as far removed from death as possible. What Schoenbeck helps us to see is that life is never more intense than when we a facing that "final entrance." Out of these stories also spills another secret: that life is also more intense for those who engage themselves with dying people.

Why is this information important for us to know? Regardless of our background and knowledge, those of us who treat patients and those of us who face the loss of loved ones tend to think of death as the enemy, if not to be overcome—obviously a losing battle is ever there was one— then certainly to be staved off as long as possible. Schoenbeck's stories help us appreciate a different perspective, of death as experience, death as journey. She urges us not to get so preoccupied with our heroic life-prolonging measures that we overlook what is happening to our patients and loved ones. We on this side of the threshold can only see death as exit; but suppose it is also an entrance?

Schoenbeck's message to us—professionals and family alike—is to take heed of these folks on the threshold of death and to attend closely to the visions they see and the stories they tell. For sooner or later, each of us must be ready when the curtain rises on our own final entrance.

—Bruce Greyson, M.D., Professor of Psychiatric Medicine, University of Virginia Health Sciences Center, Charlottesville, Virginia; Editor, *Journal of Near-Death Studies;* and Director of Research, International Association of Near-Death Studies.

Preface

Few things are more feared than death. Death makes us question. Death makes us cry. Experiences with death haunt some people. Thoughts of death torture others. Nothing is more painful than the sense of loss we feel when someone we love dies. Death is a big part of life.

Although death has been around just about as long as life has, much less is well known about the dying process. People want a picture of what dying is like.

The packaging of death has changed dramatically in recent decades. Advances in technology have allowed people to arrive at the edge of death, only to be pulled back through medical intervention. Because people now receive vital treatment so quickly, their mental faculties often are not impaired. They are returned to life and can tell stories that in the past had been lost either to death, to permanent brain damage, or, perhaps, to fear of telling the tale.

Those who have returned give vivid reports of the realm that co-exists with our physical world. This book presents the penultimate of all life experiences—the edge of death. Through the glimpses provided by these death episodes, it is possible to formulate a picture of what dying is like. This book offers a view of death from two perspectives—from the professional who cares at the bedside when patients die and also from people who have been clinically "lost" to death, only to return to life again.

Many of the stories disclosed in this book were derived from the author's clinical work and study of near-death experiences (NDEs). This book also draws from the experiences of other health care professionals—doctors, nurses, emergency medical technicians, paramedics—who regularly witness the life-death juncture. It is through the eyes of many that the author has been able to assemble the material presented here.

There are commonalities people experience when close to death. These are related in this book. The most frequently occurring characteristics of the near-death experiences are heard again and again in stories people tell.

Some stories in this book are about people being in spirit form outside their bodies. Earthly visits of people who have just died are retold by those the deceased visited. People recount watching dying family members talk to dead relatives as if the deceased were in the same room. There are reports from people who lived to describe how they watched from above as emergency teams pronounced them dead. Some stories wherein patients predict the hour of their death make it very believable that, at times, people know when they are going to die.

Beliefs about death influence a person's reaction to those who say they have had near-death experiences. Some people do not believe in near-death experiences. Some people think there is nothing—NO THING—after death. Rather, death is the final chapter; the book, as it were, is finished. Others believe that death is part of a natural process, and that at least some health care today is nothing more than interference in that process. Many believe that as people die, they return to visit, sometimes in a different form. And some believe that no one is truly dead as long as the person is remembered by someone.

It is often a mystery to us how we have come to know and believe in certain things. Beliefs are like guests who come up to a door. They come in only if the host opens the door and invites them in. Otherwise they are turned away unable to enter. Readers are invited to search in these pages for what they believe to be truth. All are invited to question, challenge, and expand their knowledge and beliefs after reading what people report here.

There is growing recognition in our country that near-death experiences are real events for the people who experience them. Many Americans who can attain everything material are now turning more attention to the spiritual rather than acquisitive aspects of their existence.

Albert Einstein believed that the most beautiful thing we can experience is the mysterious, which he called the source of all true art and science. The mystery of the near-death experience is open to anyone willing to accept the belief that people's stories about their experiences at death are reality.

To ensure confidentiality and anonymity, stories and quotes are presented as composites attributed to no specific person. The author thanks those who related their experiences of the edge of death.

Susan L. Schoenbeck

To The Reader

If we have been pleased with life,
then we should not be displeased with death
since it comes from the hand of the same Master.
—MICHELANGELO

Ask people who have had a close brush with death, "Do you believe in life after death?" They reply, "I don't just believe. I know."

This book has evolved from caring for and listening to people at the edge of death and to those who have died and come back. These pages are not written to say that near-death and deathbed experiences are indisputable. Rather, these stories are brought to you so that you may know what many people earnestly say exists beyond this life.

I came to be interested in the phenonmenon of life-after-death many years ago when I was working in an intensive care unit (ICU) for open-heart surgery patients. In those days, the outcome of these procedures was unpredictable and the tension was high even on the best of days. I was a new graduate nurse and this story comes from one of the first shifts where I was in charge of the ICU.

A woman in ICU who had triple valve surgery was encountering frequent intervals of cardiac arrest. Being a novice I was jittery anyhow, but when her heart and breathing stopped, I frantically called for help while I started cardiopulmonary resuscitation (CPR). I alternated giving her chest compressions and breaths. I was near tears and was getting desperate as I worked over her. All of a sudden, she opened her eyes and said in a very clear voice, "Sue, don't worry. I'm back."

This patient later told me that when I was doing CPR, she had been experiencing a peaceful trip down a long tunnel. But she had turned around and reentered my world. She never explained what made her come back, but I often think she hurried because she saw how panicked I was back there at the earthly end of the tunnel. Did she want to help me out? Was she working with me to come back? That was years ago and she has long since made her journey without turning back; if I ever get a chance, I would like to ask her . . . what made you come back?

Today I work in a nursing home where every day is filled with life and death. We staff have familylike relationships with the residents. Few occupations offer such a telescopic view into the hearts and lives of others.

Days in health care are physically exhausting. Days are also emotionally exhausting because caregivers care so much.

I overheard a very special nursing assistant being asked by a visitor, "How can you work in a place like this where people cannot remember your name—where some people are not in touch with the real world around them—where everyone needs so much help just to get bathed, toileted, and dressed? Don't you get discouraged? Don't you get depressed?"

The nursing assistant replied, "Actually I love these people. I look past their old bodies, their wrinkles, and their confusion. I see their very soul."

We human beings tend to see ourselves as physical beings. We are not primarily a body housing a mind and spirit, but a spirit animating, for a time, a body with a mind. When the body and mind wear out and are gone, the spirit—that is you and I—remains. Our bodies are fragile vessels holding the essence of who we are. Man does not just have a spirit. Man *is* a spirit.

The word spirit comes from the Latin *spiritus*, which means breath. This derivation implies that the spirit is an essential part of being . . . in fact, it is the essence of a person's being. One cannot exist without breath. Once cannot exist without spirit. The spirit is the innermost part of a person . . . a force that pervades a person's entire character. Spirit is the very "geist" of a person—the core of who that person is. The body and mind are, so to speak, the overcoat that the spiritual core wears.

I believe that, just as the meaningfulness of our human existence is based on the uniqueness and singularity of each of us, so is our spiritual existence based on the uniqueness and singularity of our spirit. There is nobody like you. There is no spirit like you.

To my colleagues who read this, I ask you to please think back over the times you have been with people at the end of life, or those whose lives you have saved. What were these people saying as they neared the edge? Were there clues being given about where they had been or what they had just experienced? Did you listen and hear what they said? Were you open to the real meaning of their stories or were you preoccupied by the heroic measures you were administering?

To fellow nurses and students of nursing who peruse these stories, I appeal to you to sharpen your skills of observation. As Florence Nightingale (1860) stated, "But if you cannot get the habit of observation one way or other, you had better give up being a nurse, for it is not your calling, however kind and anxious you may be." There is a spirit within everybody with which you may connect and nurture. You must, however, be open to seeing and hearing what exists beyond our world.

I hope you come to share my sense of awe when dealing with the process of dying. Please contemplate your connection. Let what you know about death enrich your caring for life. You can then make moments surrounding death comforting. You can make death not only a symptom to be treated but a life event to be cherished. Only then will human caring, despite the omnipresence of technology, dominate this final life experience. And you will meet death with peace and understanding.

—*Susan L. Schoenbeck*

CHAPTER ONE

Death is a Life Event

If you deal with the dying,
they will give you life.

Our nation can and does take advantage of new technology. And we are able to deliver this advanced care at record speed. The result is that, today, we are faced with an increasing number of elderly. Our elderly live on far beyond what was experienced generations before, although their bodies are battered and worn by time and use.

The preceding decades have brought a change in our handling of the death event. Advances in knowledge and medical practice measures have allowed quick decisions to be made to maximize treatment and even to delay death. As it became possible to do so, death gradually became viewed as a symptom to be treated and, in fact, to be treated no matter what the cost.

People now question whether the quality of health care can be measured solely by the great number of people who survive the most tragic of illness and accident. Rather, many propose that health care should be judged by the number of people who live on, for however long, with a sense of well-being and dignity. The elderly do not just want well bodies. They want, and we want for them, good health, good life, and feelings of honor and worth.

Health is not merely the absence of disease symptoms. It is a state of human dignity. We are becoming a nation that increasingly places value on the quality of life even as life closes. Our goal no longer can be just to add years to a person's life. We want now to ensure that there is quality in those years.

Health care professionals are now challenged to treat death as a life event. The public implores us to interface the omnipresence of medical machinery, tests, and treatments with human caring. We now ask ourselves not only what disease a person has, but also who is the person with the disease.

Death is not new to any of us. We know it as a physical process. Most of the time we can mark the moment when it occurs. But dying is a spiritual process as well. This side of death is not as readily measured and has largely escaped description. It is the spiritual side of the death process that is the subject matter of this book.

People have unfailing beliefs about death that come mainly from their upbringing and experience. Most of us formulate our first approach to death by observing our family mourn the loss of loved ones. Religions instruct us as to what we should believe about death. According to a survey, a majority of Americans believe there is life after death.

Many of us have been touched closely by death. We have lost people we loved, and yet we still avoid the topic of death as if by avoiding it we can deny its existence. Our human nature allows us to think that death will not happen to us until our own end is so near that it grabs control of our total attention.

For a very long time, science has gotten away with the view that what we cannot prove does not exist. Yet we all know the scientific method does not deliver all of the answers. Albert Einstein (Einstein, 1930) said, "There are emanations that are still unknown to us. Do you remember how electrical currents and 'unseen waves' were laughed at? The knowledge about man is still in its infancy."

Things happen all around us that we cannot understand or describe. Because science cannot discern these phenomena or explain them in writing or formula, does not mean they do not exist. I venture to say there is much that exists beyond our realm of knowledge. There are things that will be measured and described in the future that now are unthinkable to us. We are constantly amazed by the "discovery" of phenomena hidden to us before yet, nevertheless, present all the time. The earth was not flat during the many centuries when all men believed it was.

So as we grow in experience, we realize the scientific method cannot tell us everything. We become aware that all ways of knowing are important. We grow up and learn that textbooks do not have all the answers. And some of our most profound learning has come from people with whom we have associated. It follows then that if we want to know more about the human experience, we should put aside our preconceptions and listen to people. To know more about death as a life event, we must be willing to hear the perceptions of persons who have experienced the other side. Listening is an important way of learning. By listening, we can be open to the mysteries and meanings in what people are telling us and decide what we believe to be true.

People have taught me a lot. The very ill have told me when they were going to die and how I could help them be ready. Some who passed into clinical death and returned have told me what dying is really like. I believe the living have much to learn from the dying.

It is my hope that someday the wonders of science and medicine will be balanced with the needs of the human spirit. We can begin this marriage of body and soul by opening our minds to the awesome possibilities that edge-of-death stories present to each of us, in growing spiritually ourselves and in giving care to those who are dying and comfort to those who are left behind.

Death within Life

The idea that a person lives beyond death has been a part of all major civilizations. The Neanderthals believed the dead lived on in some kind of mysterious spirit body. Therefore, they buried their dead with supplies they would need in the afterlife. There are reports of people who were brought purposely to the edge of death in ancient times and pulled back so that they could tell of their journey.

A Historical Perspective

Long ago, death was an experience sought by elite young men who had been chosen to enter the priesthood. To be brought near-death was considered the highest of initiation rites. These candidates were brought near-death through use of mind-altering plant potions and physical tortures. Their experience was functionally identical to today's near-death experience, only deliberately induced. They later reported that, as death approached, their existence became a spiritual form outside of their physical bodies. They told of rising out of their bodies and going through a tunnel. They told of a light that met them. Each received a dramatic and unmistakable demonstration of the reality that a soul can journey beyond its physical body. The priest candidates learned that death is not an end.

Death is not a period but a comma in the story of life. Death is a transition, not a termination.

Many researchers have related experiences at the edge of death. The first documented account of near-death experience in scientific literature appeared in 1892 (Fremit, 1989). A Swiss geologist named Albert Heim summarized the near-death experiences of thirty people who fell while climbing in the Alps. These climbers reported increased clarity and speed of thought, life reviews and peacefulness.

There are common elements routinely included in descriptions of near-death experiences. These components of the near-death experience have been verified by literally millions of people who have gone to the other side and returned to tell about their "death."

The Final Entrance

We often say that all the world's a stage. If that is true, it is from this stage that we make our final entrance. The near-death experience is a powerful spiritual experience of undetermined origin. It typically occurs when a person is close to death or in a situation of intense physical or psychological danger. Listed next are the common features encountered when one journeys beyond life, as told by the people who experienced them.

The order of these near-death experience elements is not rigid. For example, some people see the being of light before leaving their physical bodies and others see it after their spirits have gone through a tunnel. Not every person has or remembers and reports having each characteristic.

Sense of peace and well-being

During a near-death experience, a person is detached from physical life. The person feels comfortable. No pain or other unpleasant bodily sensations are felt. People report joy, warmth, and comfort. Many say they feel secure, "as if they came home."

People report feeling connected to a higher power and being part of a universe. They feel they have all knowledge.

Floating of spirit above body

During the near-death event, people find themselves floating in another form above their bodies. They look down and see what is going on. They can hear the words people in the immediate area are saying. They may see an image of themselves below as their bodies lay in clinical death. For example, a car accident victim may see others pulling their body from wreckage. Heart attack victims may watch as passersby perform CPR on them. People tell stories of watching their own emergency surgery from a vantage point floating above the operating table. Often a humming or buzzing sound is heard as they soar in spirit forms outside their physical bodies.

Tunnel

People report moving very quickly through a cylinder-like space. This tunnel is described as a dark and empty region. Children sometimes say they are scared as they enter the tunnel but this fear goes away quickly.

There is bright, enveloping light at the end of the tunnel. Sometimes the buzzing or humming continues in the tunnel.

Time

Some people report that time either speeds up or slows down during the event. It is not an uncomfortable change, merely different.

Being of light

People meet a light that they describe as golden. The light surrounds them. They say the light has a personality. This "being of light" is said to be loving and forgiving. Often near-death experiencers say they are encompassed by the light and feel like a child cradled in the warmth and protection of a parent's arms. As Kubler-Ross (1991) verifies from her talks with the dying, God is not punishing. No one is an outcast.

Review of deeds

When individuals enter the light, there is an instant playback of important events in their lives. Questions are asked. People who have gone over and come back tell of similar questions such as: What have you done with your life? Whom did you love? Who loved you the most? What events made you grow? How did you use your talents? Is anyone better off because of you? Were you a forgiving person? What is the worst thing you ever did? When were you hurt the most? This life review is non-judgmental. It is conducted in a peaceful, loving manner by the "light being" and others gathered around.

The border

A barrier is reached. Someone decides whether the person will remain or return. There are often others, frequently deceased family or friends, present at this time. The dead are kind and welcoming. Although the person may want to stay, there is a push to return to the earthly world.

People do not always know why the decision is made for them to go back. Many times, the near-death experiencer is told that young children, friends, or family members need the dying person to return to life. The person may be told to go back to help someone else or to accomplish a certain task. Other times the person is not told a reason but just told to return.

Some people are called back into their bodies by someone in the room where they were experiencing clinical death. After having a NDE, a doctor said to me,"I was about to go out of the corner of the room where I had been hovering above my body watching the emergency procedures being done, when I heard my wife call my name. Her pleading pulled me back to life."

Guide

No one dies alone. People report that loving beings hover around them at death. Many people tell of guides who help them on their journeys. These individuals are kind and gentle.

Often, persons will report that a relative or close friend was the guide who met them and helped them to understand what was happening. The guide is frequently the one that tells the person to return.

Some people say guides wear white robes. Others say they are bedecked in white with gold trim. Some death experiencers describe the guides as formless. Guides say they are messengers and helpers of a Higher Being.

Beautiful Scenes

All experiencers say the topography is luxuriously verdant. They report delicate and shifting hues of color. They say the atmosphere is like translucent clouds. People come back talking of gardens, rolling hills, meadows, lush forests, lakes and music. A dying patient said to his nurse, "I pity you. The sky is not as blue for you as it is for me."

People describe the other side in different ways. This should come as no surprise to anyone since people can look at the same thing in this world and describe it in different ways. How we view the world is often a reflection of both how things are and who we are. According to the Talmud, we see things not as they are. Rather, we see things as we are. Witness the picture on the opposite page. What do you see?

Some people say this sketch is of a duck. Others are certain a rabbit is pictured. Is one viewer right and the other in error? Or can people truly see truth differently?

Descartes said, of truth and error, that it is important "firmly to retain the resolution never to judge where the truth is not clearly known." Whether this sketch is a duck or rabbit all depends on how you look at things. We are led by our experiences to look at things in certain ways.

This is much like the story of the five people who met by the bank of a river. The runner saw the river as water to quench his thirst. The farmer believed the river to be irrigation for crops.

The sportsman viewed the river as an arena to prove his skills. The child found it to be a great swimming hole. The old and wise man recognized the river as a reflection of nature's peace.

We can ask ourselves, if one substance such as the river can be seen in so many ways, how can any thing have one true, inherent meaning? Is this why some people view the world as heaven and others as hell? Budda said, "Nothing is as it appears." Indeed there is no objective reality. We should not find it strange that people describe afterlife in different ways.

Return to body

In a sudden burst, people find themselves "popped" back into their physical bodies. When this happens they start to once again sense the feelings of the physical body, such as pain and cold.

People are sometimes angry when recovering from clinical death in the emergency room. They may say they are mad that they are now in pain whereas they had just experienced comfort in the life beyond.

Message: Do not fear death

The most outstanding outcome for persons who have experienced death is that they no longer fear death. Death, they say, is not the end as they had thought. Rather, death is the final entrance to a wonderfully spiritual world. Near-death experiencers often try to tell others that death is not the end of existence.

Individuals may have some or all of these parts of the near-death experience. The parts may not happen or be remembered in this order. The longer one is clinically dead, the more likely that person is to experience many of these aspects of the near-death experience.

It is estimated that one-third of all people who come close to death have a near-death experience. Millions of Americans say they've had near-death events (Greyson, 1986). No one knows why some people have near-death experiences while others do not. There are men and women, children and adults, professionals and blue-collar workers, and religious and non-religious people. There is no one group, culture, race, religion, age, or sex that seems to have more near-death experiences than others.

Children tell stories of the tunnel and light and seeing religious or family figures. They can describe the efforts medical personnel make to bring them back to life. Generally, children do not report that they have a life review or that time has sped up or slowed down. Children may report momentary fright when they enter the tunnel; this feeling goes away quickly.

Distressing Near-Death Experiences

While most near-death experiencers universally report positive events, there are sporadic accounts of experiences similar to the near-death event yet incorporating frightening components.

Out of the hundreds of near-death stories I have heard, only three have been distressing. Two are presented in this book. Other researchers and clinicians report a similar paucity.

Distressing near-death events may not be reported as often as positive ones for several reasons. One, distressing events may be rare. Two, people may fear reporting them. A person may not want to relive the bad event by telling it. A person may not want others to characterize them as bad if their near-death event was full of hellish components. Three, clinicians and researchers may be uncomfortable in hearing, and therefore not fully open to accepting, negative versions.

Greyson and Bush (1992) describe three distinct types of distressing near-death experiences. The first type, "terrifying" near-death experience, is characterized by fear of being taken out of one's body. The person may feel loss of control. The terrifying near-death experience may evolve into a pleasant event with the features of bright light, tunnel, etc.

A second distressing near-death event has been labeled "nonexistence or eternal void." In this experience the person hears voices mockingly saying life on earth was an illusion. Malicious laughing is heard. This event does not convert into a peaceful near-death experience.

The third type of distressing near-death experience, called "Hellish Imagery," depicts demons and grotesques beings. People report moaning, crying, and wailing. This event does not convert into a peaceful near-death experience.

Although the number of reported cases is small, researchers are interested in interviewing people who have distressing near-death events. Persons experiencing distressing near-death experiences are encouraged to contact Dr. Bruce Greyson at the University of Virginia Health Sciences Center, Charlottesville, Virginia.

Inner Experience and Outward Changes

A Death blow is a Life blow to Some
Who 'till they died, did not alive become
Who had they lived had died but when
They died, Vitality begun.
—EMILY DICKINSON

What is Emily Dickinson saying? A brush with death brings about changes in people. These changes in people, after a near-death experience, have been strikingly similar. A brush with death may teach a person to live differently from before.

The near-death experience is a significant life event that may serve to initiate a transition process for the individual who experiences it such that, after having a near-death experience, a person's beliefs and goals may not be the same. This inner experience leads to outward changes.

Reduced Fear of Death

Near-death experiencers share common personal and interpersonal aftereffects. In addition to a certainty in life after death, experiencers report a reduction in the fear of death. Perhaps the biggest reason people fear death is that they do not know they are unconditionally loved. The near-death event shows the experiencer unconditional acceptance, thus erasing the fear of death.

Spiritual Development

The experiencer, now less fearful of death, may also become less fearful of life. Realizing the impermanence of possessions, the experiencer may give up the pursuit of material possessions and focus more on personal spiritual growth. To work on development of that part of one's being which doesn't die—the spirit—becomes vitally important.

Experiencers are not known to become more religious after a near-death event. This characteristic is often disappointing to the clergy. Many experiencers talk of an increased awareness of the presence of God yet emphasize the universals of religion rather than any particular religious dogma. More often than not the experiencer tells me that God is too big for any one religion. More often than not, the agnostic comes to believe in a Higher Power. Witness this prayer a sixteen-year-old wrote as he experienced the dying process.

UNBELIEVER'S PRAYER
Almighty God
forgive me for my agnosticism
For I shall try to keep it gentle, not cynical,
nor a bad influence.
And O!
if Thou art truly in the heavens,
accept my gratitude
for all Thy gifts
and I shall try
to fight the good fight. Amen
—JOHN GUNTHER, JR. (Gunther, 1949)

Often the experiencer assumes a strong need to be of service to society. The person may change occupations to accomplish this. Commonly, the near-death experiencer switches from a profit-oriented to a service-oriented career.

Or the person, after the enlightenment brought through the near-death experience, may become more attuned to helping those people who are part of his everyday life. You'll hear experiencers echo, "I'm nicer now. Little things that used to bother me about certain people and life in general just don't seem to rile me up any more. I take things as they come and make an effort to go more than half way."

Aloneness

This person who has a near-death experience may need some time and solitude to weigh what has happened. Giving up the beauty and comfort of the world beyond is an enormous adjustment. Usually the experiencer needs a span of time to assimilate the profoundness of what has occurred.

Many who have had a near-death experience feel confused about how to put this phenomenon into words. They also feel people listening to their story might think they are crazy. Sometimes a person will start to tell and the listener will block attempts by saying such happenings are not real. I've had people tell me about their near-death experience right after the event while they were still in the intensive care unit. Others have told me their stories many years later.

A few years ago I gave talk about near-death experiences to a group of lay people. The day after, I received a phone call from a woman who wanted to tell me about her near-death experience that happened 76 years before. The elderly woman said when she first told her mother about this event when it happened, in 1916, the mother warned her to not tell others. And so she, until then, did not feel she could unburden herself of the story.

People flock to share what has happened to them when they know someone believes and will listen. You can sense the relief from aloneness the near-death experiencer feels when their story is heard.

Heightened Psychic Abilities

Although near-death experience does not occur more often in people with professed psychic abilities, near-death experiencers often turn up with heightened psychic abilities after the event. Experiencers may report they are able to:

- Communicate by unexplainable means: Telepathy.
- Be in the exact location and/or time in relationship to other events or people: Synchronicity.
- Know something before it happens: Precognition; and
- Have knowledge of events that cannot be attributed to logical deduction or reading of cues in the environment: Clairvoyance.

Life Changes

As you review these aftereffects, recall that near-death events can happen and do happen to anyone of any age, religion, and walk of life.

What this means is that any person having a close encounter with death may suddenly act and think differently than the person did before. These changes may translate into significant interpersonal communication problems, for "there's a new guy at home."

Mr. Kelly was a patient of mine who had a near-death experience during his second heart attack. This event, in his words, made him "sit up and listen." He decided he would no longer work his usual sixty-hour business week. He would cut back and enjoy hobbies as he had always meant to do. He would also find ways to help the less fortunate.

This change would surely mean less income from fewer sales. It would impact his lifestyle. There would be no more fancy cars and fewer fancy vacations. He needed to tell his new wife what changes he envisioned. Mr. Kelly imagined this would strain their relationship. Therefore he sought my advice.

As he lay in his ICU bed, we role-played how Mr. Kelly would tell his family. He practiced his responses to questions we could guess they would pose. Back and forth we tossed the words he would use to explain the phenomenal event that made him feel changed. Mr Kelly practiced saying aloud, "I feel different than I did before. I crossed a line into heaven and came back. I want to do different things now that I am back. I know I was a guy who gave you lots of fancy things. I still love you. That has not changed. I still want to give you things—my time and me. I want to share myself with you." Mr. Kelly left the ICU a man whose life would be altered by the near-death experience. Because of the event, his life spun off in a different direction. He hoped his family would understand.

If millions of Americans have had near-death experiences, it is reasonable to question why they have not all taken what they have learned and made this world a better place. This is a question I am often asked. Why aren't there millions of spiritually-charged people out there doing good works?

The answer, is human nature. One, the process of change is difficult and may takes years if it is accomplished at all. The near-death experience, for sure, is one way people are assisted in learning more about themselves and their purpose in life. But it is not the only clue we meet in life that screams out at us to look up and down at ourselves and our lives and repair the damage we have done. And it is not the only clue or insight we ignore.

Changing ourselves and our lives is hard and risky work. Our lives can be like an old pair of shoes—kind of loose and sloppy, but comfortable. We are uncertain how a new pair would feel—surely not as comfortable at first. We hold onto the old shoes, even if they have holes in the soles, because we do not want to go through the trouble and discomfort involved in changing to a new pair. Even though the pain would be transient, we resist.

Change is hard. We hold on to the familiar—the old tried and true. Even though we become aware that there are holes in our souls, we may not expend our energies to repair them. Repair takes work. Repair takes effort. Repair can be painful for us and also adversely affect those around us. That is why, although near-death experiencers may gain understanding into who they are and what their purpose is in life, they may not change outwardly at all. They stay in the past busy with all their old responsibilities and frenetic activities that provide excuses for their not taking the time and effort to advance their spiritual development and service to mankind.

In the words of Bob Dylan, "He who is not busy being born is busy dying." Some near-death experiencers find the effort and pain of growth and change too monumental to pursue. These experiencers back off and hide their new feelings within their old selves. They do not evolve into more spiritually whole people. They become the living dead.

Secondly, the opportunity to be heard is not always there for near-death experiencers. Health care workers are themselves just starting to understand death and the dying process. Near-death experiencers need attentive ears to help sort out, to sift and winnow, to weigh what has happened.

Doctors and nurses, emergency workers, and families may miss that the near-death experience has occured. They often are misguided by a person's stoicism and reticence. Health care workers often do not give opportunity for discussion. Yet near-death experiencers are always hoping someone will see beneath their disguise and open up conversation about what has happened to them.

The near-death experiencer seeks out someone who can look at the event from the experiencer's perspective—someone who understands that the ways things have appeared to the near-death experiencer is that person's reality. The experiencer seeks out someone who is open to understanding and believing. Once you've read the stories in this book—this person may be you. Life is a constant interplay of divine forces and human actions. Biological destiny and environment are materials that can be shaped by the human spirit. Your understanding may help someone gracefully integrate the near-death experience into their life.

CHAPTER TWO

Spirits Among Us

Spiritual growth comes in ways and at times least expected.

Most of us have been brought up to believe that if we have a spirit while on earth, it is fixed within our physical body. We have difficulty believing that a spirit could roam outside of the body. Thus, many people believe that when life is done, any spirit which may have co-existed with our body goes to heaven, or somewhere else, but does not maintain an existence that is in any way related to our earthly world.

Many others feel that, just as ideas exist without physical form, spirits may, in fact, occupy, without a physical body, space on earth as people do. People who have experienced existence as spirits say they felt that they were present in this world, but just not within their bodily form. They had out-of-body experiences.

Where do people go when they are out of their physical bodies and are existing only as a spiritual form? They tell interesting stories of movement to ceilings and corners of rooms, and through walls. Some travel great distances, while others stay close to home. For example, people may have out-of-body experiences at home, in hospitals, and above accident scenes. Some stay in the room where emergency teams work on their bodies. Others visit home scenes far from the site where they are "dying." Some spirits go out and find people they want to be with one last time. These people return to their bodies and can share their adventures as a spirit. They confirm that no one saw their spirit forms.

Human Being is just one manifestation of being. It is known that out-of-body spiritual existence commonly occurs with a critical illness or in a situation of grave psychological danger. Journeys out of the body may also be done at will. Robert Monroe (1971, 1994), an everyday businessman, has logged his adventures as a spirit in space beyond his body. He conducted laboratory supervised exits from his body and describes the process he used to leave his body, his travel in a spiritual form, and the logistics he encountered in order to return to his physical form.

The disembodied spirit, it appears, visits whomever it pleases. The living, too, tell of being visited by spirits of the dead. Widows and widowers, and sons and daughters, commonly report having felt the presence of, seen, heard, or been touched by the deceased. Death does not necessarily erase a relationship. It may simply place it in a different context.

People tell stories of going about their normal in-body existence, and unexpectedly running into people who were in spirit form. For example, many people have told me stories of "knowing" and "feeling" the death of someone before they were told of that person's death. These people say the reason they knew a death occurred was that the disembodied spirit of the dying person visited them one last time just as that person was leaving this earthly life. People who have had such visits often have had a hard time telling others about these encounters. They worried that people might say they were just making it up, trying to make others think they were special. Or they thought people will believe they were crazy. They wondered, "Why me?" Was there a reason this spirit came to visit? Their stories make one think there may be a supreme force connecting us all—some of us more closely than others. This earth may be more crowded than it would appear.

There are commonalities in stories of spirits among us:

- Spirits may exist without physical form.
- Spirits may view and hear clearly what is happening around them.
- Spirits may sense when an out-of-body experience is about to occur.
- Spirits may travel near or far.
- Spirits may visit the living.
- Spirits may bring messages.
- Spirits may be called back into their bodies by those who love them.
- Spirits may sense when death is near.
- Spiritual presence may be sensed by the living.
- Spiritual connections are poignant.

The stories that follow convey a sense of presence of spirit in each of us. We have come to know there is another dimension of existence. We are more than body and mind. Our true essence lies in the spirit that interconnects us with all forms of the living and dead. Encounters with spirits suggest a spirit from which we cannot separate ourselves. These stories sensitize us to that sacred spirit in each of us.

Stories show wide agreement that spirit survives death. The puzzzle remains as to whether the body is resurrected to be with the spirit. Elizabeth Kubler-Ross (1991), in *On Life After Death,* states her belief that a person's spirit may temporarily abide, after death, in an ethereal body that is whole and healthy. This heavenly body later is laid aside, she says, as one becomes comfortable in one's spiritual form.

Take a moment to picture the bodies you have seen die: flesh rotted with cancer; bones so brittle breakage has occurred here, there, and everywhere; nerves eaten away by disease so muscles can no longer move legs nor arms; eyes that do not see; ears that do not hear; mouths that cannot speak; lungs that gasp to catch a breath. Does anyone believe a just and kind God would say, "Bring that body along with you?"

Stories witness that spirits are among us and touch our lives. Stories lead us to recognize spiritual selves that lie within us all. There is a spirit in each of us that nothing, not even death, can destroy.

Shelly's Walk

Often when I give a lecture about death and dying, nurses come up and tell me of the experiences they have had when someone has died. Some tell of patients they cared for. Others share stories about the deaths of siblings, parents, and other relatives. For each one who recounts their experience, it seems, some peace of mind is gained.

Karla is a nurse who told me this story about her sister, Shelly. In this narrative you will find that Karla senses her sister's spirit leave her body at death. Shelly's husband tells how Shelly's spirit traveled to meet him. These are Karla's words.

Shelly was my sister. I was with her when she died. I will tell you how I witnessed Shelly's spirit separate from her body and go to meet her husband.

That February afternoon when Shelly died, there was a fresh snowfall. I had promised Al, her husband, that I would stay with her while he went out to do some errands. He trusted me to be with her as her days dwindled; cancer had invaded her body and was winning a painful war.

The old log cabin where Shelly and Al lived was picturesque as the midwinter snow fell. An unblemished layer of white covered the lawn and drive; even the trees seemed to have received an equal share of the painting of white flakes. Shelly lay quite still, confined to a bed in the main room. We talked. She sat up for a few minutes to have some tea and a muffin I baked for her. After eating, she became too tired to talk. She lay down. A restlessness grew in her as the afternoon wore on. She guardedly moved from side to side. She did not complain but I could tell it was becoming harder for her to catch her breath. Sometimes her breaths were not much more than small gasps. She tossed and turned, pushing the covers away from her. She whispered to me that she needed fresh air and asked me to open the window. I did. The winter air did not seem to chill her.

Then I heard her say something directed to Al, even though he had not yet returned. "Al," she whispered, "thanks for being with me." She spoke quietly and calmly. Peacefulness came over her face. She no longer struggled to change position on the bed. She did not stir. Her breathing became more shallow and there were long pauses during which she did not seem to breathe at all. Shelly's restlessness had turned into peacefulness.

At the same time I heard Al's car come up the drive, I could see Shelly fade away. By the time he got into the house she was no longer breathing. Al embraced Shelly, talked to her and laid her lifeless body back on the sheets.

When I left the cabin later that day, I noticed two sets of footprints in the snow leading from the house to where Al had parked the car. No one had left the house since the last snowfall. Only Al had come home. When I pointed to the tracks in the snow, Al was not at all surprised. "As I came home up the drive, Shelly's spirit came to meet me," he said, without hesitation in his voice. There was no other explanation and we let it go at that.

The Visit

In this story, an emergency room nurse speaks of how she felt the spiritual presence of her brother as he was dying far away.

I was 28 and my brother Brian was just 26 years old when his plane was shot down. The Air Force said Brian had no time to evacuate before the explosion. His body was recovered from the crash site. I know, however, that Brian's spirit remains. It visited me the night they found his body.

My husband Jeff wanted me to come upstairs to bed but the plot of the mystery I was reading was exciting. I wanted to know what would happen to the heroine next so I couldn't put the book down. I kept reading. I told my husband Jeff I'd be to bed soon. But, after a while, I fell asleep on the couch.

When I awoke two hours later, the lights were still on. I should not have felt frightened. But I was scared and checked under the couch and in the closets looking for someone. I did not know who. It seemed like someone was lurking in the room. I even looked up to check the cathedral ceiling of the room. But I saw no one. I heard nothing. As I changed into my rose flannel nightgown, a feeling of sadness, unlike any I've ever known, overcame me. I did not know why I had this dismal feeling, but it weighed heavily, and gloom trailed me as I crawled into my bed. "Something's wrong," I was thinking as I fell into sleep.

Jeff woke me early the next morning to say that he had taken a call from my dad. My dad wanted me to call him back right away. Jeff did not know why. But I knew something was terribly wrong. I hurriedly dialed Dad's number. Dad said Brian, my brother, had died during the night. The plane Brian was piloting in Asia had crashed.

I added back the time difference and calculated that Brian had died the same time I awoke the night before. I believe Brian came to my house to see me on his last night on earth.

Watching CPR

An intensive care unit nurse shares here a valuable lesson she learned and carries with her every day as she cares for critically ill patients. The nurse says she was startled when she learned people could go out of their bodies, float above her, and watch everything she was doing to them as an ICU nurse. A teenager taught her that spirits can move and see and hear clearly.

The patient was a sixteen-year-old. He was a member of our town's high school basketball team and he fit a nightly schedule of practice into his already busy study and social calendar.

It was after a late practice that he was approached by a young boy. The boy attempted to rob the basketball player and, in the struggle that followed, the sixteen-year-old went down with a stab wound to the abdomen. He lost consciousness by the time paramedics arrived. They began emergency measures, cared for the wound, and transported the boy. On arrival in our emergency department, he was still unconscious and was near-death. The resident on call tried to restart the boy's heart. CPR was continued as he was wheeled to the operating room. Although it was close, the boy lived.

The resident who had treated him in the emergency room and I were both present when he woke up. He immediately recognized the doctor even though he had not met him before the knifing. I was at the young man's bedside when he looked up at the doctor and said, emphatically, "I know you. You kept hitting me on the chest the night of the stabbing. I saw what you did. I was floating above, watching." He went on to describe the operating room and the operation as only someone who was there could do. He knew what was done to him and how the room was set up. The young man said he looked down from a position in the corner of the room. He said he didn't feel anything but he saw everything.

Whenever I am in a life-and-death situation where someone is critical, do I ever wonder where that person is? You bet. I believe the person could be right above watching what I am doing.

I Saw Him Drinking

Lorraine told me she had chronic pain due to arthritis. In order to lessen her discomfort, she chose to undergo a knee replacement. At the time of her surgery, she was well acquainted with leaving her pain-ridden body and floating comfortably above it.

Lorraine had been regularly leaving her body for about twenty years. She said she always stayed at home, but her spirit moved from room to room in the house.

This story illustrates how some people are able to escape painful bodily sensations and float around and about in a spirit form. For the time they are out of their bodies, they are pain free.

This night Lorraine was in a lot of pain. The surgery performed on her knee made for suffering beyond belief. Bone pain . . . everyone had said bone pain was the worst. Lorraine agreed.

Her husband drank a lot. He never drank in public. Only at home, when the sun went down, he reached for the cabinet of liquor above the refrigerator. Most nights their kids were asleep by then. Most nights she also went to bed not wanting to see him guzzle from a bottle of 80 proof as a baby sucks milk.

Lorraine had crutched up to the second floor bedroom, took the pain medication, and tried to relax. It was not easy for her to relax with her leg immobilized in a thick, heavy brace.

Her husband came and asked what he could do. "Just sit here with me until I fall asleep," Lorraine said. "I can relax if you just sit here with me. Then I'll sleep." But Lorraine's husband had no time for this. Liquor called him. He stayed one minute and then went downstairs. She was not relaxed. She could not sleep.

Later Lorraine's spirit lifted out of her body and followed him, hauntingly, down to the kitchen. There, from a position floating at ceiling height, she saw what held more power for him than any concern for her. He took the bottle, as if it were his life's blood, and drank.

Everyone, I believe, wants and needs someone they can count on to be with them during the bad times as well as the good. She needed him to stay by her—to be with her. He was with himself.

The separation of Lorraine's spirit from her body that night finally convinced her to seek help to get strong so she could get a divorce and start a new life. She already was by herself. She could not feel more alone than she felt that night being with him. And, maybe, she thought, she could find someone to be with her, body, mind, and spirit.

My Husband's Ghost

The diagnosis was grave. She had metastatic breast cancer. The cancer had spread. The social worker who told me this story went to the patient's bedside in hopes of alleviating a bit the patient's fear of dying. But this patient told the social worker she wasn't at all afraid to die. She said she believed people who passed on could keep contact with the living. The social worker recounted his patient's story about how deceased spirits visit the living.

"My husband died when the children were two, four, and five," the patient told me. "But he came to see me regularly. He came to me often when the kids were sick, to give me advice and help, I guess."

The woman, now in her 50s, said that her deceased spouse's spirit spoke to her in a normal voice. His words were not just thoughts going through her mind, but were, she said, "like regular sounds." She said, "Once he ordered me to take my youngest daughter to the hospital. When I took her, I found out that she was very sick and that it had been critical that I had not delayed getting her there. I would not have taken her had he not been so insistent."

She went on to say, "For seven years after he died, he visited each Christmas. We all smelled his tobacco smoke as we gathered around the tree. And each year an ornament would fall off—-the same one each year—and I believe it was his little sign he was there with us."

Heaven Sent

Jill Kaufman was a nurse who always talked to her patients, even those who did not respond to her—patients whom other people wrote off because they were in comas. Jill remembered her first nursing instructor's words: "Hearing is the last sense to go." Jill's story tells how she observed a dying patient talk to an already deceased relative.

I believe patients in comas might hear me. But I was surprised when Bertha, an eighty-year-old cancer patient admitted in a coma, started talking, not only to me but also to people clearly not present in the room.

Every day when I came on shift, I told Bertha my name. This went on for three weeks without any visible sign that Bertha knew who I was. One evening, as I repositioned Bertha to make her more comfortable, she startled me by suddenly speaking clearly and saying "Hi" and calling me by name, "Miss Kaufman."

Then Bertha returned her focus to a spot in the upper corner of the room. A childlike voice came out of the old woman. She cried, "Mommy" and spoke as if her mother was there in the corner. "Mommy, stay with me," Bertha pleaded. "I am ready," she added softly.

Within moments of this happening, Bertha's family came to visit. I told the family that it appeared Bertha had been talking to her mother. The family was pleased. They said that Bertha had been very close to her mother. Bertha died shortly thereafter.

This story illustrates how nursing personnel can help families recognize when a patient is transitioning into death.

She Left

Paula is a nurse who takes her profession seriously and does a very good job. She is experienced and has worked with dying patients for many years. But she believes in balance and tries to keep thoughts of work, however melancholy, separate from her home life.

Paula, however, was unable to keep work separate from home when a dying patient made a visit to Paula's home. Paula tells this story.

I had cared for Joan since she arrived on our unit. We all knew there was nothing more we could do but comfort her. There was no hope for recovery. I became close to her. We talked a lot about her life, her dreams, and what was to come. We did the little things that made her happy . . . like have vanilla ice cream in the afternoon. I know we became friends.

But it still surprised me when I smelled her scent at my house. I was just doing little household chores when a smell I knew to be Joan's came out of nowhere. It would not be so significant except that when I reported to work, I found out that Joan died at the same time that the scent came upon me at my home.

I Was His Godchild

When I give talks about death and dying, people sometimes cry. And later, these same people line up at the speech breaktime and afterwards to tell me their stories. They often struggle for words to describe the visions and emotions they have often held silent for years. It's hard to tell others you think you've been visited by a dead person. But, after listening to my talk, the audience knows that I believe such things can happen. It happened to me.

I still remember the evening well. I was a graduate student at the time, working on a manuscript that was due the next day. The desk was cluttered with pieces of paper. I was struggling to put my words and ideas onto paper.

Usually when I'm under the gun to get something finished, I'm focused and a bit irritable. I work hard to get things done on time and I do things well.

But my mind kept turning to thoughts of my uncle Dick. I had last seen him at my brother's wedding fourteen years previously. I know that I had surprised him that day. I had always been a gangly, awkward kid for whom he, as my godfather, did special things, such as buy gifts no one else could afford. He always took time to talk with me. He was interested in my growing up. On the day of my brother's wedding, I could tell that he was happy to hear about my college experience. He asked lots of questions. What are the classes like? Do you have friends?

I stopped typing that night and thought, maybe for five minutes, of Dick and of what a significant part he had played in my growing up. Then I felt less tense and harried and I went back to my paper writing.

The phone rang an hour later. It was my mom, Dick's sister. She said she had bad news. I said I bet I could guess—Dick had passed on. I didn't tell her how I knew. I didn't say Dick's spirit passed through to see me. I think she just felt it was a lucky guess. I had felt Dick's presence. I felt his spirit checking up on me one more time as he left. Now I know what "passing on" really means. There's a process to leaving this earth. You are not here one moment and gone the next. This life is a passage to the next.

Child's Play

I listen to people a lot. Oftentimes, I jump the gun and respond to their words too quickly because my mind reads what others want to say before they can express themselves. People say I have an antenna that goes beyond normal receptivity. I believe this extra sense was born in my experiences in out-of-body travel which started as a very young child. When out of my body, I could see and hear what was going on in the room where I floated. I grew up not bound to this world. I learned, in small increments, to trust that my experience in the world beyond was real and valid. I know all the talk about Light and Love is true because I have been there.

Sometimes we wonder why there is pain and suffering. We, whose bodies are less than perfect, see and feel people gawk, questioning the futility of our lives. Some people cannot fathom how we can be ful- filled and happy. Yet living with disease can teach one many things unknown to others. I am grateful for what illness has taught me. I started my learning as a child.

My first recollection of being in spirit form was as a very young child. I had polio. Every night as I lay down to sleep, my parents put a brace on my leg to keep it straight in hopes that someday I would walk like others. I remember the clicking sound of the heavy metal parts as the brace was attached to my leg. My parents placed it on carefully, caringly. Maybe that's why I am a nurse.

Lying there, unable to move side to side because of the heavi- ness of the metal, I stared at the ceiling. I had a lot of pain from the base of my ankles to the base of my spine. So sleep did not come easy. That's when I started to travel. My spirit rolled out and upward from my body.

My spirit would often leave my physical self and float above my body until the pain subsided and I could return to sleep. I was never afraid. Rather, I felt good . . . no pain . . . no iron brace holding me down. From a vantage point floating above my bed,

I could see my little sister lying there asleep curled up with the blankets she had hogged from me, and for which I had not strength to fight back.

At first leaving my body and existing in a spirit form happened quickly—all at once. But as the years went on, I could sense the very beginning of this gradually unfolding process when my spirit let go and lifted up and out of my physical body. Sometimes I would consciously choose to leave my body for the peace and comfort I experienced outside it.

This evening I remember as clearly as if it was yesterday. I was about nine years old. I was a Brownie scout and my troop had spent weeks with endless spools of cord weaving planter baskets for our mothers for Mother's Day. I was especially proud of mine. My mother was so special and I was so happy to make this surprise gift for her.

It was dark, cold, and rainy when I left school to walk the three blocks to my house. My baskets were complete with shoots of new little plants. My legs hurt as they always did when the weather was humid and cold. Since I fell often, I was scared I would drop this present I had worked so hard on and had such wonderful visions of delivering to my mother.

It was then that I consciously willed to get out of my body. It felt like Isaiah described: "And He will raise you up on Eagle's wings, bear you on the breadth of dawn, make you shine like the sun, and hold you in the palm of His hand." I watched from a place above in the dark as my little body walked home, never missing a step. I saw myself walking. But I wasn't in those walking feet. I was floating above my physical body in a spiritual form. I could see I was being carried on another spirit's shoulders. And I felt no pain. I popped back into my body when I got to the doorstep.

I know there is a place for all of us where there is no hurt. I know my body is something I use now but I can exist without it.

And I know there are other spirits—helpful and good spirits—out there too.

Sister and Brother

If you have ever been a brother or a sister, you can remember times when you have been in sync with your sibling and also times when you've been polarized at opposite sides of an argument. Some brothers and sisters connect in life and even in the stages immediately beyond life. This is Patty's story in her words. It reminds us that spiritual presence may be sensed by the living.

I was twelve years old. My brother was getting dressed to pick up his prom date. My family would not let him get ready alone. We all took part. Dad picked up the tux. Mom got the camera loaded. I took the corsage from the refrigerator so it would not be forgotten. Each of us oohed and aahed when Rick came out wearing his tux. Mom and dad snapped a picture as I threw him his date's flowers.

We—mom, dad and I—piled into the station wagon to follow Rick"s Chevy Impala. "Hey you guys, you forgot the dog," yelled Rick. I ran back to get our old dog "Scotch" while Rick sped away down the driveway. I'll never know if Rick really thought Scotch should be part of this family affair or whether he was just delaying our car so he could go off on his own.

After the excitement of a photo session at Sue's parents' house, Rick and his date climbed into the front seat to head to the formal parade that would start at the center of town and go out to the high school. Dad pulled along side Rick's Impala so we could have a closer look at the radiant couple. Rick was not racing. He took his time keeping pace with dad. Our cars were side-by-side, going parallel down the two lanes of the road.

My brother then took a long moment and looked into my eyes and mouthed the words, "Good-bye, love ya, Patty." He waved.

His gesture wasn't a quick, "See you later, kid." Rather, the whole scene seemed drawn out—surreal—like a supernatural happening. And then the prom king and his queen turned onto Main Street. Dad, mom, and I went straight home.

I remember waking up about 1:30 a.m. I didn't know what awoke me. Everything was quiet. I tossed a while and heard the chimes on the living room clock ring 2:00 a.m. before I fell back asleep.

The call from the emergency room came about 3:00 a.m. My dad took it. Rick was dead. They tried to save them both. They tried but both Rick and Sue were dead.

I feel as if I said my last good-bye to Rick when I waved back to him from the station wagon. I believe Rick somehow sensed his saying good-bye and waving were more than ordinary courtesy. I feel he somehow knew then it was a special goodbye. Now when I replay what happened, I see Rick's face and feel how his final glance pierced deep into my soul.

Why did I awake at 1:30 a.m.—the time Rick died? Was his spirit passing through one more time on its way? I wonder.

Now I am a nurse and I work in an emergency room. When someone says, "I'm dying," I believe the person may know ahead of the rest of us. I believe Rick knew. Paramedics who bring patients to the hospital where I work have told me they routinely deal with patients who, on the way in, say, "My time's up." and almost always they prove themselves right.

They Didn't Know I Was There

Patients who are, for moments, clinically dead, do sometimes tell how their spirit form was pulled back into their body when a loved one, such as their spouse, entreated them to "come back." This phenomenon happens to children as well as adults. I can attest to this because I've experienced it. This is the story of the tremendous pull my mother's love had on me as a spirit when I was a child.

"Sue's dead! Sue's dead!" I didn't think until then that anyone could run full speed and still scream so loudly at the top of her lungs. Although my sister, Kris, was heading away from me, I could still hear her yelling as clearly as if she were standing right over me. The kid showed more spunk than I had previously thought she had.

Kris screamed as she ran from the garage to the house. Our garage opened onto an alley. A path had been worn on the grass that led from the back of the garage to the back steps of the house. I can picture it all now. I could see it all then.

Yes, I could "see" what was happening although I lay unconscious on the garage floor. Defying rules of safety like any other ten year old, I had been using the two cars parked side-by-side in the garage as "parallel bars." Unfortunately, I was not what you'd call a practiced or perfect gymnast, and one big swing left me with a bump on the back of my head, knocked out cold on the concrete garage floor.

From a place above where I floated, I could see my sprawled out skinny, scrawny, pale body. I could even see through the garage wall and watched my sister running and screaming. I was not afraid. I was comfortable. I felt no pain. I was calm. I felt no urgency. Time seemed slowed down.

The neighbor boy arrived first. "Oh, no," I thought to myself. "Him to the rescue!" The last person I ever wanted to touch me! (You get picky when time slows down, you feel good and somehow know things will be all right.) I was lucky he didn't know CPR. He just looked down at me. And I, floating above, looked down at him looking down at me.

I knew I wanted my mother. I kept saying over and over in my mind, "Momma, Momma." But the crowd that grew around me was saying, "She's not breathing. Give her air," and all those other things people learn from TV. I could see everything below me. I saw everyone looking down at me. I stayed above them all. They didn't know I was up there.

My mother finally arrived and as soon as I saw her bend down over my body lying on the concrete floor and heard her voice say "Susie, Susie," I knew it was time to pop back in my body. And I did. She was right above me and gave me a hug I still remember today. She pulled me back. A mother's love can pull one back into one's body. She knew I was there.

I Remember Well

The morning after giving a talk about near-death experiences to a group of elderly people living in a retirement complex, I received an early call from an 87-year-old woman who wanted to meet me for lunch. Martha said she could hardly wait to talk to me. I broke at 11:00 for lunch. Martha was vibrant as she relayed this story of how the spirit of her father talked to her sister. She had been afraid to tell anyone for more than three-quarters of a century.

It was 1916 but, still today, in 1993, "I remember it well," Martha said without reservation. When it happened, my mother said we were not to tell anyone; no one would have believed us then. "I am so happy to tell this story now."

Seventy-seven years had passed but Martha recalled the event with exactness. She was only ten years old when her father died. He had been troubled by heart problems. He had chest pain often. Martha's mother told all the children to be quiet while papa rested. Martha and her sister, Lizzy, went outside to play so they would not disturb him.

They were chasing their cat, Charlie. It was hot and the sun's sweltering rays beat down on the girls. Lizzy, though sixteen years old, was not as fast as Martha because she had heart problems. Martha careened past the porch and grabbed Charlie just as the cat was ready to hide under the front porch. The shade under the porch offered a good spot to rest. Martha crawled under the porch and lay flat on the ground nestling her head comfortably on Charlie's furry back.

Lizzy was consumed by the search for Martha and Charlie. She checked behind the woodpile and shed, in the root cellar, and between each currant bush that lined the garden wall. Exhausted but determined, Lizzy started to run circles around the house in hopes of catching the cat and finding Martha. Lizzy collapsed in a heap on the lawn as she started the fourth lap.

Martha, alert to all Lizzy's running in circles, was concerned when she didn't hear Lizzy's voice saying, "Here, Charlie." Thinking Lizzy gave up the chase and the game was over, Martha crawled out of hiding, at the same time letting Charlie run free again.

When Martha found the two, Charlie was licking Lizzy's face that lay flat in the grass. She couldn't arouse Lizzy. Martha called her mother. Her mother came outside and held Lizzy up in her arms. Lizzy had fainted but "came to" quickly.

"Papa said I had to come back," said Lizzy. She said she was following papa down a road in a beautiful place when he turned to her and told her to return. "You must go back, Lizzy," were his words.

Papa never woke up from his nap. Mother went into the bedroom and we could hear her sobbing. She couldn't wake him. Doctor Bennett said papa died peacefully in his sleep and we should be grateful he didn't have pain any more. Mother kept crying. She was lonely without papa. Lizzy and Martha found her crying a lot.

Lizzy was haunted by her "dream" of Papa telling her to go back. She talked to her Mother and Martha about it. Her mother said, "Lizzy, don't you tell no one. You would be casting pearls before the swine. No one would believe a girl's story like that. People would laugh and make fun of you."

So now, 77 years later, it's finally okay to tell this story. Lizzy is dead now. But Martha said Lizzy believed their Papa came to her as his spirit left that hot summer day. When her time to die was near, Lizzy did not fear death. She faced it head on and said she was sure papa would meet her there. She knew she was going back to a place she had been before with papa. Lizzy always said "her dream" made her know that death leads to a wonderful place. Martha believes her. Today she tells others about Lizzy's experience; some people believe her and others do not. Martha knows the story to be a true pearl of wisdom.

Mind Games?

A mother was quick to tell me this story of her daughter's miscarriage. It seemed she sought from me validation that people from this world can connect with spirits in the world beyond, that spirits do visit the living. She told me how her daughter, Peggy had "an experience" with her grandmother who was dead.

Peggy waited to get pregnant until she and Bob felt they could feed another mouth. All the time Bob was in graduate school, money was sparse. He received a meager amount of grant money, studying the relationship between intimacy and commitment in elderly couples. Peggy's job shelving books at the campus library paid for rent, food, transportation, and little else.

So as Bob assumed his position as associate professor at a small Midwestern college, Peggy prepared for the birth of their first, long-awaited child. Peggy's mom was involved, too. Together they stripped the veneer from Peggy's baby crib and revarnished it. They pieced a "neuter" quilt and hand-sewed the seams as Peggy's mom talked of the exciting life and times raising her children. Peggy had three older sisters. Each had already finished their child-producing years. Peggy's child would be born at least six years after the last of her sisters' children.

Peggy was a runner. Her doctor said there was no need to cut back on her miles until she was uncomfortable or further along in the pregnancy. Peggy was just, by all measures, three and a half months pregnant.

The day was hot. An egg could fry on the pavement, thought Peggy as she ran the last blocks to home. She grabbed a magazine and poured herself some lemonaide before she slouched in the wicker porch chair that overlooked the patch of flowers she had planted in their tiny backyard.

Peggy's not sure if she was just thinking or dreaming. But she remembers well the content. She saw her grandmother sitting in a rocking chair holding a newborn baby girl. Peggy could tell it was a girl because it was swaddled in a rose colored blanket and wearing a bow. Peggy's grandmother said, "Do not worry, Peggy, I will take care of her." Then the scene faded.

Two months had passed before this scene came to Peggy's mind again. She was now lying in the hospital after surgery to clean out her womb. She had spontaneously aborted a baby girl during the night. Peggy spoke to her mother about seeing her grandmother holding a baby girl and telling her she would take care of the child. "What does this mean?" Peggy asked, wanting some direction from her mother. Neither woman has the answer. But there is a sense of peace each feels in thinking Peggy's grandmother could be caring for her child in a life beyond this.

Appearances

Do the dead appear to children as well as adults? It may seem so if we believe the story Elizabeth tells. Elizabeth, a mother of a first grader, told me she was sure her daughter had met her great aunt. But her Great Aunt Betty had been dead seven years when the two met. Her daughter Rachel was six. This story tells how spirits can bring messages.

It wasn't until Rachel had to put together a "photo family tree" for a class project that Rachel's experience with Aunt Betty came to light. When Elizabeth and her young daughter dug through a box of old photos, Rachel pulled out a dog-eared picture of a woman dressed in a business suit. "Aunt Betty," she exclaimed, "She saved me."

Elizabeth had no idea what Rachel was talking about. Great Aunt Betty had been the independent woman of the family. She took a job overseas as an employee of a bank that had a home office in Chicago. She wore a suit most days, unlike the majority of women of that day. Betty was killed in a train accident before Rachel was born. Elizabeth could not remember telling Rachel about Great Aunt Betty.

Rachel said she remembered going off alone away from the other children during a family reunion. Elizabeth said she recalled clearly the day Rachel described to her. The cousins had gathered with all their children for a reunion at the home of Elizabeth's mother . . . There was a lot of homemade food. Everyone had brought dishes to pass. Elizabeth recalled being absorbed in conversations to catch up on all that was happening with the cousins with whom she had been very close as a child but who now were spread all over the United States.

As the adults ate and talked, the young children of the cousins either toddled or crawled around the big expanse of the house. Older children were cajoled into watching that the younger ones didn't get into trouble. Grandma's house was not childproof; her collection of antique figurines were like a mine field that young hands could blow to smithereens.

Rachel recalled that she was rambling toward the open basement stairway when a lady wearing a blue suit caught her, pulled her up off the floor into her arms, and set her down again to walk the opposite way, away from the stairs. The woman had told Rachel she was "Aunt Betty" and "Aunt Betty didn't want Rachel to get hurt." Rachel said Aunt Betty told her that only she could see Aunt Betty that the other people in the house could not see her. Aunt Betty said she just came "to save Rachel from an accident."

Elizabeth to this day does not know how Rachel could have known about Great Aunt Betty unless Betty had appeared to save Rachel and to spare the family from experiencing the tragedy of another family member dying in an accident.

Old Dead and New Dead

Some nurses are open channels to the spiritual side of existence. Marguerite is such a nurse. People who know Marguerite know she's a nurse who listens and respects what patients tell her. Maybe that's why patients open up to her and tell her of their visits with the dead. Marguerite had this story to share with her colleagues after a hectic shift working in the intensive care unit.

I was working the night shift in a cardiac ICU. One of my primary patients that shift was Carol, an elderly "with-it" woman admitted for congestive heart failure. Carol was in Room 2.

In Room 3, next to Carol's, was Joe. Joe was in his early sixties. Twice he had cardiac bypass surgery. The nurses knew him well. But, as always, they were taken back when Joe suffered a cardiac arrest at 2:10 a.m. Everyone went into action doing compressions, getting an airway in, and giving emergency drugs.

When Carol put her light on, I turned over my responsibilities to another nurse and went to Room 2. Carol was alert and sitting up in bed. She said, "I know you are going to think I'm crazy, but I just saw my mother." She seemed startled. Her mother had died many years before. I told her about other patients who had been in the cardiac unit and said they had been visited by people who had died before. We talked for a while. I shared stories people had told me about the visits with relatives and friends who had died before. When I left, Carol seemed very happy that she had seen her mom.

In the meantime, in Room 2, Joe had expired. Staff had discontinued emergency treatments by the time I returned to the scene. Later we learned that Joe had a ventricular aneurysm that had burst.

As we nurses sat down to chart all the happenings of the previous couple hours, we discussed what had gone on. When I told about Carol seeing her mother, other nurses shared stories of their patients' experiences with visitors from the dead. This night made the group wonder: Is there is some connection—an opening or channel—between previous dead and new dead? Did Carol's mother, an "Old-Dead," come to help Joe, a "New-Dead," go over to the other side?

Sometimes I sense you near me
Although you have gone away.
You enter my life
As if it were yesterday
When you were alive.
I feel the soul of you
Pulling my thoughts astray.
As if we are together in an endless day.
Your spirit still touches me.

CHAPTER THREE

Deathbed Talks

The willing suspension of disbelief unveils the world we see.

We have learned of the existence of the disembodied spirit through stories of people who have been clinically dead and later have returned to life to tell of travel in a spirit form. The disembodied spirit concept has also been reinforced through deathbed stories the dying tell us. The dying say they see and hear spirits who, by all accounts of the patient, have come to guide them into another existence.

Until I became a nurse I did not know what people were like as they approached the end of their lives. Because I was trained to start CPR if I found a patient not breathing and with no heartbeat, I was alert at all times for signs that I would be the unlucky one to first happen upon a death. After I shared the experience of the dying many times, I concluded that death is not always a sudden occurrence. In many cases, death is preceded by recognizable events. And you will see, no one dies alone.

The terminally ill often predict with firmness and accuracy that suggests they know their death is coming soon. We professionals, despite all of the lab tests and readings from monitors, are often surprised when the final crisis actually arrives.

The dying often say they see and talk to people who have died before. Some observers say that seeing and talking to deceased relatives at the time of death may just be dreams. After all, dreams are a rehash of what is going on in our lives. It seems natural, then, that the dying may think a lot about their relatives who have died and, reasonably, could dream of family who have gone before.

For this reason, many health care workers who observe the dying say these people are hallucinating. A nurse wrote this note in a patient's chart to describe his status:. "The patient says he was in heaven today and talked to family members who had died before. He seems happy to tell me this. He is in and out of being oriented to place and time. He talks to people conversationally who I can see are not present. Plan to check on him frequently for hallucinations."

This patient died shortly after these notes were made. If you look at the charts of many patients who have been labeled as hallucinating, you will find that numerous individuals were at the edge of death as borne out by their demise within hours or days.

No longer am I surprised when a patient near-death becomes suddenly alert and coherent with an elevated mood. Nurses tell stories of patients who become happier just as health care workers are becoming frantic in efforts to save them. Nurses often "catch" patients at the edge of death speaking to what appear to be deceased relatives. Some of the dying report that they have even talked with God. At first this is surprising, until you see enough of it.

Several recurring themes emerge from deathbed talks. The dying talk about:

- Focusing one's gaze on a corner at ceiling height.
- Being in the presence of the dead; for example, "Mom and Pop are here with me.
- Preparing and, later, being ready to travel; saying for example, "I'll be ready soon. I'm coming."
- Being in another world; stating for example, "I see the light. It is so beautiful. I see angels waiting for me."
- Being able to control the time of death; for example, "What is the date?" and then dying on the chosen, meaningful date.
- Resisting death until given permission to cross over.
- Becoming lucid one last time.

A person can find meaning in life up to and through the death event. It is not unusual for family members and nurses to report that a dying person opens their eyes and smiles an incredibly peaceful and happy-looking smile and, then, without saying a word, dies. For some, this smile is a sign family had been waiting for—a sign that tells those who are left behind that the dying person is all right—all right, just somewhere else.

Communion

When I was a coronary care unit (CCU) nurse, I had a patient who knew better than I that death was coming. Lora Keller, a probable heart attack victim, was admitted to the coronary care unit where I worked. She was settled into a two-bed room and hooked up to a machine that showed her heart beat on a TV monitor. I had inserted an intravenous medication line in case she would need emergency drugs. We were running the usual blood tests to confirm the suspected diagnosis. Nothing particularly unusual appeared to be happening in this case. I later learned that Mrs. Keller was preparing herself to die.

One night shift I did notice that Mrs. Keller was not sleeping well. At 2:30 a.m., I went in and took her blood pressure, and everything measured all right. Her heart rhythm had not changed at all.

She calmly asked me if I could arrange for her to be given communion. Her words were not the pleadings of a desperate person. Mrs. Keller was alert, coherent, and polite as she made her request. She looked me in the eyes and reached out her hand to me when she asked me to call the priest. Somehow I knew this was an important time, that this woman with the silver grey hair and bright blue eyes did not want to wait for morning rounds when Father Mike came to offer the sacrament. I sensed the woman had her reasons and, although I did not know what they were, I felt compelled to carry out her wishes.

Father Mike was 73 years old, but he never missed a day of rounds to offer communion. I telephoned him. "Tell her I'll be there in the morning," he said politely but firmly. I said, "She wants you now, Father." "But she's not on the seriously ill (SI) list, is she?," he questioned. I had to admit that she wasn't. "Then I'll see her during morning rounds," said Father Mike.

"I just put her on the seriously ill list," were the words that came out of my mouth as I wrote "Lora Keller" on the listing of SI patients. It startled me that I could be so bold. But somehow I knew this was important. "Oh, well, I'll be over," Father Mike conceded.

Lora Keller received communion about 3:30 that morning. She smiled and slept afterward. At 6:30 a.m., she blew a hole in her heart the size of a half dollar. No amount of CPR or drug therapy could bring her back. She died.

Reviewing the deathbed scene and putting things together, I look back at my time with Lora Keller and am happy that she had her last wish. I am not happy that I subjected her to all the resuscitation methods I knew. I started CPR. I led the team that gave her every appropriate cardiac drug from the emergency cart. I will always regret my role although I realize, at that time, it was the thing to do. I am glad now people can say "no" to CPR if they want to go without such measures. I am grateful that somehow she knew she was dying and was able to let me help her fashion her final entrance.

Janie's Grandpa

Janie had graduated from nursing school five years before and was working in the obstetrical delivery unit of a large metropolitan hospital. Because she was the only relative with any medical training, she was often asked to explain what was going on, in layman's terms, when family members became sick. This particular day was no different except that Janie, unfamiliar with how dying people often talk to their deceased relatives and friends as they prepare to pass over, had no clue her grandfather was dying. Only years later did she look back on the event and realize she had been witness to her grandfather's deathbed talk. Janie describes this experience.

My mom called to tell me she checked in with the nursing home and the nurse said Grandpa Jake was getting worse. Would I go to visit please and then call her back and tell her how he was doing? Even though I lived a two-hour drive from my grandfather, how could I not go?

When I arrived, I knew that I had made the right decision. Grandpa looked pale as he slept in the tiny room provided in the Medicare section of the nursing home. Grandpa did not stir, so I read a magazine left on the windowsill. It was almost an hour before my grandfather awoke.

I watched, surprised, as Grandpa Jake sat up and began to talk, not to me, but to absolutely no one visibly present; at least no one that I could see. Grandpa was looking at a corner of the room by the ceiling. "I will be with you soon dear. I will be with you soon," he said. His conversation went on. "I'm almost ready. I want to be with you."

Grandpa Jake didn't even notice me until I loudly cleared my throat. Grandpa Jake then first recognized he had a visitor. "Oh, Janie, I'm so glad you are here." I was worried that my grandfather was hallucinating. I asked Grandpa Jake to whom he was talking. "Why, it's your grandmother," Grandpa Jake said with assurance. "She is back to get me." I, taken aback, asked if grandma came to visit often. "Oh, lately she has been coming, Janie. She is coming to get me."

I thought as I drove home that Grandpa's talk was all gibberish. His mind was wandering back to old times. When I arrived home, I called my mother to tell her about the visit. My mother said the nursing home had called about an hour earlier; the nurse told her Grandpa Jake had died peacefully in his sleep soon after I left.

Looking through a Window

Joan was a nursing student on summer break from college. Since she had experience caring for patients, she agreed to spend her three-month vacation living in rural Iowa with her Aunt Lynne who was terminally ill with a brain tumor.

Joan was prepared, through her clinical experiences in a hospital, to provide baths, intravenous narcotic medication, and other comfort measures. When she took the job, Joan felt equipped to handle everything, even Lynne's expected death.

Aunt Lynne died just two weeks before Joan was to return to school for her senior year. What she learned that summer about the dying process established a foundation for Joan to listen carefully and observe closely patient conversations when they were near-death. Joan tells of her Aunt gazing into a corner of the room while talking to someone not physically present.

I remember Aunt Lynne woke up from a nap two days before her death. I was sitting in a chair next to her bed. She was on a steady dose of narcotics and had been experiencing periods of confusion, but at this particular time her mind was clear. She knew who she was, who I was, where she was, and the time of day.

Aunt Lynne looked around the room and then focused on an empty corner. She began to have a quiet conversation with "someone" she saw there. I don't recall her exact words but I do remember she was not frightened by this "person." It seemed quite a natural conversation for her.

Afterward, when I asked her to whom she had been talking, she said, "Joan." I did not know a Joan. At the time, I was uncomfortable. I was not frightened or disturbed, but uneasy like a child looking through a candy store window . . . wanting to grab a piece of chocolate but knowing that I could not reach through the glass. I could not enter Aunt Lynne's experience. I sensed there was something or someone very real there, but in a place I could not reach. I could only observe Aunt Lynne talking to someone who was somewhere I could not be or see.

At the funeral, all the cousins talked about our memories of Aunt Lynne. Uncle Paul joked that Aunt Lynne and her cousin Joan were probably raising the dickens in heaven just like they had done as kids on the farm. Joan was the name that Aunt Lynne called out when she spoke on her death bed to the person I could not see.

Upon graduation, I took a position on an oncology hospice unit where I can be comforting, respecting the connection between people of this world and their loved ones in a world beyond.

Mom and Pop

This story comes from Doreen, a nurse who began to revisit and relook at some experiences she had with dying patients after she heard, at a nursing conference, about deathbed talks. Doreen speaks candidly.

It's sometimes hard to talk about this because in a way I feel guilty. I was not with this patient when she died. I did do CPR when I found her not breathing and pulseless. But when I did CPR, I sensed she had already left.

Mildred was over 90 years old. She was admitted for congestive heart failure. I checked on her hourly or more because her blood pressure was unstable.

When I entered the room, I asked Mildred how she was. I expected to get a "comfortable" or "not so good" answer. Instead what she said surprised me. "Oh, I'm fine," she said calmly. "Mom and Pop are sitting here with me." There was no one present except Mildred and me.

Each time I came in, Mildred insisted her parents were there with her. When making my rounds just before entering her room, I could hear her saying, "I'm ready to go. I'm done waiting." She continued to talk to her parents while still answering my questions and following my directions as I put the blood pressure cuff on her arm. But by the end of the shift, Mildred had died.

I learned only later that dying patients may have conversations with relatives on the other side. Maybe if I had believed at the time that the dying actually talk to people who have already gone on in death, I could have been more helpful to Mildred. I might have said "I'm happy your Mom and Dad are here." I might have said "Good bye, see you later." I might have asked if she really wanted CPR to be done.

I Saw the Spirit in Her

This story depicts a dying woman telling her friends she is ready to die and, then, at the moment of death, smiling.

I was one of a group of long time friends gathered at the bedside of Dorothy. Some of us had known her since childhood. Cancer had taken over her body and brought unbearable pain to her every movement. She needed us and one of us was always there for her in the end . . . to get her a drink . . . to turn the pillow . . . to help her toilet . . . to give her more pain medicine. She was unable to do these things for herself. She had become incapable of existing without us and so each of us took turns helping the past three months.

One afternoon, we were surprised when Dorothy, before unable to move without assistance, suddenly sat straight up, and raised her arms above her head. She began to talk to the people she said were four horsemen who were waiting for her. She talked about the beauty she saw in a light. She said the light gave love. Dorothy said the heavens opened and "they" sat and waited for her.

The look on her face was beautiful. She was radiant now even though scourged by the effects of cancer and its treatment. A peacefulness came over Dorothy's face and then she quietly and gently lay back onto the bed while telling "the horsemen" she was ready to go. She died moments later.

We friends have been unalterably changed through this experience with Dorothy. We believe a spiritual world does connect with us. We saw and felt Dorothy interact with a spiritual presence in another world. She appeared at peace as she knowingly passed out of this life.

They Didn't Know My Grandfather

I watched a lot of cowboy shows when I grew up. On TV, they always died with their boots on, the way they wanted. "Life support" was a shot of brandy at the end to ease the transition. I wish it had been this way for my Grandpa. Let me tell you his story which exemplifies how the dying can know and tell others death is imminent.

My grandfather celebrated every life event with a drink—all holidays, all weddings, all birthdays. And when he retired from the railroad at age 74, every day became a holiday. Each afternoon he drank peppermint schnapps with beer chasers. His hard and honest way of living made his hour of death even more poignant to me. This is how he died.

Grandpa was talking to his oldest daughter, my mother, who sat by his bed in his room at home. Grandpa had been sick a long time and his body lay weak and pale. His urine was dark and foul smelling. His breaths were shallow; he made little effort to take air in. Death was expected. He had lain so quiet for so long that everyone thought he would pass away in his sleep. But, this day, with an unusual and sudden burst of energy, Grandpa lifted himself upright on the bed. He stared straight ahead and said, "Wash me; Jesus is ready for me. I need to be clean." My mother helped him wash up. After he was so prepared, he lay back down. His breathing slowed to a stop and then started up again. Purplish-blue blotches came over his chalky-white skin. He looked as if he was dying.

My mother called an ambulance to take Grandfather to the hospital because this was the big city where no longer did people die at home. The ambulance people immediately started CPR though my mother wanted them to let him die.

The paramedics didn't know my grandfather. At 84, after a full life and a sure sense of what he was entering, he would not have wanted their CPR. Grandpa was going to a new life. This was a day to celebrate. I know Grandfather would have just wanted one more chaser. Since they didn't offer him that, he quickly left.

Dying at Home

More and more people are opting today to die at home. Hospitals are costly and the bustling, high-tech environment too often uncaring. This story comes from a public health nurse, one who cares for people in their homes. Again, we see how a dying person can enliven just before death. This story also illustrates a theme caregivers often report, i.e. that of a widow or widower following within weeks or months their beloved spouse into death.

I was a nurse for Dave, a man sent home from the hospital to die. Dave was fifty-three. He was tired and had little strength to talk with me when I came to change his dressing. His wife was always close by. They shared glances and touched often. I could tell they were on the same wave length. The love and mutual respect each had for the other glowed. She spoke for him to tell me he wanted this or that. And he nodded, "yes" if it was his wish. I was awestruck by their wordless communication. It seemed so natural for them.

One day, I was surprised to find Dave incredibly animated and cheerful. If not for the story his temperature, heart rate, breathing, and blood pressure told, I would have thought his condition was improved. It was the day of our most meaningful interaction. Susan, his wife, was at the store. He spoke up and told me about his life: what he had done, what pleased him, how he loved Susan. He asked me to care for Susan if something happened to him. I said I would.

Dave died without stirring in his sleep that night. His beloved wife of twenty-plus years died unexpectedly within one month despite the fact that her health had previously been good. Their son told me his mother died of loneliness and a broken heart. I think so too. I believe Susan chose to join Dave.

This public health nurse says sometimes people give up the will to live after their loved one has died. Without the drive to go on, the one left behind may succumb to an illness that may have been silently, asymptomatically present before.

I See the Angels Waiting for Me

Renee prefaced telling me about her mother's last days by saying, "I am Jewish." She said she was hesitant to tell this story to other Jewish people for fear they would think badly of her. Renee went on to

*tell about her mom who was 67 and, although Jewish, did not prac-
tice her religion. Her mother describes angels commonly reported by
the dying to be present in the next life. Seeing angels when death is
near has been reported by people of various religions. Angelic beings
seem to comfort those to whom they appear.*

Mom didn't belong to a temple. But we went to temple as
kids. At thirteen each kid in the family had a ceremonial Bar or
Bas Mitzvah. So we knew what being Jewish meant.

We were taught that death was the end of life. It was expected
that we all believe there was no heaven or hell. There was no
afterlife to think about. That's why mom's remarks surprised
me.

The cancer had weakened her so much. Mom didn't move
much anymore. When we visited her in the hospital, she opened
her eyes. We thought she recognized us. But she didn't talk to
us. She just groaned when the pain was particularly bad.

I was alone with mom. She took the medicine when the nurse
offered it. She looked up to the corner of the room and, when
the nurse left, she began to talk clearly. "I see you there," she
said. Then suddenly mom sat up. Her eyes were open wide.
She said, "Renee, I see the angels on a bench. They are making
room for me." Her voice was clear. There was no mistak-
ing what she said. It was hard to believe she was sitting up without help to hold her. It was hard to believe she was talking and
acknowledging that I was in the room with her. She had not
been in touch for so long. Yet she spoke assuredly. Her lucidity
struck me.

Mom died a day later. I believe she saw the other side.
Heaven . . . some sort of place beyond with angels . . . yes I'm
convinced it's there. Mom was so sure. I believe her.

My Daughter is Waiting

As a nurse I know it is important to take a few extra moments, even when time is limited, to talk with patients. I did so with Sara one day and she told me she had talked to and had seen her deceased daughter. Sara told me she would die soon.

"Will you miss me if I'm gone when you come back?" This was the question Sara posed, in a whisper, to me as I knelt at her wheelchair. I had stopped to talk to Sara even though I was in a rush to catch a plane to fly out to a conference. I told her I would not be at work the next couple days but other nurses would be there to care for her.

"I'm gonna miss you," she said. Sara always had something to say that made you glad to be a nurse working with her. Of course her saying she would miss me touched my heart. I know I took a deep breath and nestled down by her and smiled into her twinkling hundred-year-old eyes.

She continued talking, for she really had no idea what it was like to be late for a plane. Airports were not in her frame of reference. But she trusted me. I was part of her care team. She knew I would listen even if I was in a hurry.

Sara decided to tell me, "I saw my daughter again." Now this would not be worthy of mention except that Sara's daughter had died many years before. Sara had told me about her. She always beamed with pride when she talked of what a lovely woman her daughter had been. The two had been close in life.

"My daughter told me she has two chairs and one is for me. I will be joining her soon. She told me it is so beautiful in heaven. She looked beautiful too when I saw her. She was sitting in one of the chairs. I'll be ready to go soon. I will not be 101. God will take me before then."

I went on my trip. When I came back Sara was still there. She said she missed me. I missed her too. And I thought about her a lot while I was gone. I kept wondering if she was going to die while I was gone. I've had other patients who have talked to deceased relatives on the other side in the weeks or months near their deaths. I knew that she was being readied for death.

Sara was always calm and peaceful when she talked about dying. She knew death was just around the corner for her. Sara lived one day beyond the year she expected. She died at the age of 101.

He Lifted Up

I am a nurse at a long-term care and rehabilitation center which has a loving, professional staff. When my friend Donna told me about her brother, Joey, I knew placement in our nursing home was a good decision for him and for the family. Joey wanted to die. This story portrays a man who resisted death until he was given permission to die.

Joey had given up. He refused to eat. Life, as it was, no longer appealed to him. He was angry. He was hurt. He was pained. Donna told me she didn't know what to do.

When a young man in his twenties is diagnosed with a spinal cord tumor and paralysis results, who does know what is best to do? I only knew to tell Donna there was no right answer. She could only listen carefully to what her brother wanted, what his medical choices were, and then she could clarify options for him so he would be clear about what he wanted to do. Whatever, the future looked grim. They faced a long, hard pull.

Luckily, Donna was able to arrange for Joey to be admitted to our facility. He entered the nursing home because the hospital could do no more for him and his daily needs could not be met at home. At first he responded to his surroundings and caregivers with interest. He began to eat. One of the nurses went out to a restaurant and got him a fast food chicken dinner because that is what he wanted. Joey enjoyed interacting with staff.

Joey accepted therapies at first. A physical therapist moved his arms and legs to keep muscle tone. Occupational therapists splinted his hands to prevent contractures. Nursing assistants bathed, fed, and clothed him. He was living each day to the fullest he could.

Joey was religious. He believed in a heaven. But, after a few months when the days' activities became routine, Joey told the visiting chaplain he did not want to go on. And he told others the same by not cooperating with cares, and by refusing to eat. He talked less. He began to be lost in thought for long periods. He lost weight but refused nutritional support measures. His heart started beating in an irregular pattern.

Joey's family never left his side until he himself gave up life. They stayed and prayed by his bedside. They massaged his legs. They told Joey they loved him. They were getting tired for they had families of their own and other lives to take care of also. Donna asked when I thought Joey would die. Donna asked me why, if Joey wanted to die, did he hang on by a slim thread?

I sensed Joey was on the edge of death and needed permission to cross over. He needed to know his family was ready. I talked to Joey. I told him that his family loved him very much. I told him it was okay to leave. His family would be all right. I told him he had a very nice family who would remember him always. I was concerned about both Joey and his family—mother and brothers and sisters. Everyone was exhausted.

An evening later when I just stopped in Joey's room to say good-bye for the day, I felt a difference in the room. There was a heaviness above Joey's body. I knew his spirit was leaving. I've felt this denseness at death beds before. You become aware of the weighty presence of spirits after you meet some. I asked the family if they wanted me to call their pastor. They asked me if I thought death would be soon. I said "Yes, I think so."

Just after the pastor reached the nursing home, Joey gave up this life. Everyone had openly shared their love for Joey. Each family member had said their good-byes. I believe Joey's spirit stayed there long enough to hear his family say they would see him again in heaven.

Did I wonder if my giving Joey permission to die pushed him over the edge? Yes, of course. Do I believe in sharing that death is a viable choice when the person has no hope or will to live? Yes, indeed. Do I feel everyone was comfortable with Joey's dying? Yes, I believe so.

I Knew He Was Dying

Death was not uncommon or common to me. It happened sometimes. In my 22 years of nursing, I have seen my share. Many times patients were brought to the nursing home, where I worked, to die. I noticed how some people, just before dying, became lucid, energetic, and communicative. Such a person was Bob's father.

Bob brought his father to the nursing home knowing full well that he would die there. All he asked was that whatever his father wished be done for him. There was no hope for recovery from the cancer that spread throughout his body pushing on nerves and pressing on organs and causing unrelenting pain. There was just a son's hope that his father's last days be as best as they could be.

Bob didn't live in town. He had to jet back across the country. But he left his work and home phone numbers and the plea, "Call me when you think he is dying."

Of course all of us nurses had heard that request before—to call family when the end is near so they can visit one more time. We can promise nothing. For we may not know when the end is near. We made that clear to Bob. We could not tell for sure.

Bob's dad's condition gradually worsened. He stopped getting up for meals. He began napping more. He refused nourishments offered in between meals. He seemed depressed. His weight dropped dramatically.

The social worker assessed his depression as moderate. The nurses were concerned about his nutrition. Bob had told the nurses that his dad always loved a beer before meals but the doctor wouldn't order it. The nurses thought a beer before dinner might increase Bob's dad's appetite and, thus, strengthen him. The doctor wanted to order an antidepressant. The nurses argued that the man could be dead before the antidepressant level became adequate enough to make a difference. The dying man wanted a beer. The son wanted the nurses to get his dad whatever he wanted to make his last days good. The doctor ordered the beer. When Bob visited his dad, he joined him in a beer and dinner that we had brought into the room on trays for the two of them. We nurses took special satisfaction in seeing that meal shared.

Bob visited as often as he could. With each visit he saw a weaker and weaker father. His dad's responses were becoming more muted. He slept more. He gave up eating. He only took sips of fluid the nursing assistants offered. Bob wondered if he should stay on. Was his dad going to die now? The nurses did not know. So Bob flew home.

It was on a Sunday that I found Bob's dad sitting up in bed when I made my first rounds. He said he was hungry, although he had had no appetite for days. He was alert and oriented, although the weeks before he had been lapsing in and out of a semiconscious state. I knew this change was significant. Many nurses have seen lethargic and confused patients become coherent and active when they approach death. I called Bob and told him of the change in his father.

Now it is hard for someone who has not experienced this active lucidity that often occurs pre-death, to believe a nurse may know this means the end is near. Sheer logic would make a person believe the patient was recovering, not dying. But I've had other patients who for a short time before death—long enough to say what they wanted and good-bye—also had been uncharacteristically actively lucid. I advised Bob to fly out.

Bob was able to make it to his father's bedside before he died because I had read signs that told me death might be near. My nursing of people at the edge of death had taught me that a patient becoming suddenly lucid was one of those signs.

Minnie's Choice

I noticed a woman crying in the third row of seats as I delivered a talk about death and dying to a group of pharmacists. At the seminar's breaktime, she came and introduced herself as Jan. She said the stories I told about patients who controlled the timing of their deaths were meaningful to her. Jan went on to tell me how the information I shared validated for her that her mother chose a time to die.

Jan first told me more about the life of her mother, Minnie. Minnie was just 67 when she had a stroke while gardening. She lay there on the damp ground, weeder in hand, unable to move until Tim, the newspaper carrier, found her. And funny he did. A good worker, always on the move, always on time, Tim knew Minnie's berries would be ripened on the vine. He slipped through the back gate to snap a few into his mouth when he discovered Minnie staring up at him. Startled, Tim let out a yell. He asked Minnie what was wrong. She moved her lips a little, but no words came out. Tim was scared. He ran to the neighbors next door to get help.

Minnie spent months in the hospital. At first she was fed with a tube through her nose. When there seemed to be no hope that she'd regain her ability to swallow safely, a feeding tube was inserted in her stomach. The garden Minnie had always prided herself on withered and died.

Jan often took the train from the city out to see her mother. Jan was ever encouraging Minnie to work with the therapy people to get better. Minnie responded with mute cooperation. Therapists moved Minnie's arms and legs. Nurses lotioned her body frequently and turned her body in bed. They hoisted Minnie into a chair so she could see her surroundings. There was no response from Minnie. If she was observing, she wasn't telling anyone.

In December Jan and her brother John gathered with their families at Minnie's house. They would all make a Christmas Eve visit to the nursing home where Minnie now lived. This would be the first year the family had not enjoyed the traditional Christmas Eve feast followed by midnight mass. Minnie's husband of 51 years had died the previous winter, so everyone knew even before Minnie's stroke that Christmas would be different this year.

Jan said that Minnie had not really been the same since her husband, Edward, had died last January 7th. Oh, she still invited people over. She went through the motions of enjoying company. But there was a sadness in Minnie's eyes that her children could not help but notice. They felt some of their mother's spirit had gone with their father when he died. As teenagers, Jan and John saw a similar torture of their mother's soul. Their older brother, Jim, was killed in a freak car accident at his army base. He died, also on a January 7th, a day etched in Jan and John's memories.

Minnie changed after young Jim's death. Whenever a door opened or closed unexpectedly with no one in sight, she would say, "That's him; He's here." Jan remembered always asking, "Who's here?" And Minnie always replied, "Your brother, Jim. He's just stopped in."

When the family made their Christmas Eve visit to the nursing home, Minnie was dressed in a holiday outfit. Her hair had been styled and she looked lovely. She was sitting in a chair out on the solar porch. The children excitedly rushed to hug her. Minnie did not move. She did not speak. Although everyone chattered on about their lives like birds on a washline, Minnie was still.

In early January, Jan was surprised to get a call from a nurse saying Minnie had spoken. The nurse said this was a good sign and maybe Minnie's condition would improve. Jan was excited. "What did my mom say?," she asked. The nurse replied that Minnie had asked what day it was. And when the nurse told her, it was Wednesday, Minnie said, "No, not the day, the date." It was January 7th.

When Jan arrived at the nursing home a few hours after the nurse had called, the nurse manager of the unit met her at the front door. "I have to talk to you," she said. "I'm sorry," the nurse continued, "she died right after I talked to you." The nurse said she felt badly for getting Jan's hopes up. The nurse said she thought the words of Minnie were a start toward recovery. Jan was not angry. How could the nurses have known January 7th held such meaning for Minnie? January 7th was the date on which Minnie chose to die.

Pearl's Band

One of my friends, Clarice, told me of the conversation she over-heard her mother having the night before she died. When I explained that the dying often talk to people who have died before, and describe being in a more beautiful world beyond, Clarice decided to share this story with family and friends in the eulogy she delivered at her mother's funeral. In her tribute, she told people her mother died happily, ready to be part of a band she saw and heard playing.

Clarice's eulogy centered around her mother's love of music. In her talk she told how, being a music teacher herself, last 4th of July she brought six of her middle-school horn players to the apartment complex for the elderly where her mother lived. The group entertained while the residents followed along singing the "Star Spangled Banner" and "America, The Beautiful." Pearl beamed as the students played their instruments and she later served them ice cream and lemonade.

Pearl had played the clarinet in the community band that gave outdoor concerts weekly in the summer and indoor performances monthly the rest of the year. Her manner was dignified and stately. Years as a soloist had taught her to stand tall and carry herself with precision. She loved music. Clarice set up a VCR in Pearl's apartment so she could watch Lawrence Welk show reruns.

It was fall—a busy time of the year for Clarice with new students trying to learn to play on old school instruments. After teaching each day. she stopped on her way home to visit her mother. Clarice shared the highlights of her day and always asked what her mother had done.

This day Pearl was lying slumped in bed when Clarice arrived. Clarice let herself in with her key. Pearl complained that her head hurt. "Those damn sinuses," she moaned. Clarice offered to make her mother some soup and a sandwich.

From the kitchen, Clarice could hear humming and then words. When she returned to the bedroom with the food, she found Pearl sitting straight up in bed talking. "I know that. Sure I can play that part. I'll join you soon. It sounds beautiful," were Pearl's words.

Clarice asked Pearl if she had been singing. "Oh, yes," said Pearl. "My friend Rose came and told me we'll be playing 'Starlight Swing.' I was just remembering the melody. Rose said I'll have the solo part I like."

Pearl ate the soup and sandwich while chatting animatedly with Clarice. Clarice then finished cleaning up the kitchen and told her mother to call her if she needed anything else. Pearl asked only that Clarice give her an ice pack to place on her forehead.

There was no call from Pearl that evening. It was Clarice's brother who found Pearl's body still in bed the next day.

Clarice told me that her memory of that last evening with her mother brings much comfort. She believes there is music in the life hereafter. She's confident that Pearl has again found her band. Clarice's eulogy confirmed for others that Pearl was ready to die.

A Glimpse

As nurse in charge of the night shift, I made rounds to check out all the patients. As I walked down the hall, I heard Maria, a 92-year-old woman in kidney failure, talking aloud to someone. I went into her room because I knew no one could be there at this time of the night. Maria's eyes were focused at the upper corner of the room as if she saw someone there. I could see no one. Only Maria and I were in the room. Maria talked about joining the person to whom she was talking. "I'm coming soon," she said.

I've been a nurse a long time, so I've often seen patients talk to persons not present. The patients never seem frightened at these times. The conversations never seem hurried. I'd say when patients talk to people who are not there, the patients clearly know whom they are talking to and the dialogue is most often about the patient joining the person somewhere. These conversations occur more and more frequently as patients approach death.

I had a sense that I should spend some time with Maria that shift. Although really no direct care was ordered for her, except morning medications, I followed my instinct to be with her.

I gave her an early morning bath, cleaned up her bed, and helped her change into her favorite gown, robe, and slippers. I rubbed her favorite body lotion on her feet, arms and elbows.

Maria seemed to know that death would be arriving soon. She looked up to the corner of the room and repeated several times during that shift, "I'm almost ready." She died at 6:00 a.m.

I am glad I cared for Maria that night. Giving comfort is one of the most satisfying things I do as a nurse. It's funny how when you're in this business a long time you recognize death coming and, like the patient, you are not afraid.

Momma, are you here for me?
Momma, are you there?
I'm reaching, Momma, up to you.
Help me, draw me near.
Momma, I can see you.
Momma, you are so clear.
I'm reaching, Momma, up to you.
Help me, draw me near.

CHAPTER FOUR

When My Eyelids Open in Death

Love is accepting someone as he is.

I f you ask people what they think death is like, they will very likely say that you go out of your body and "away somewhere." Floating out of one's body at death is a widespread idea. Where do you go after leaving? Of that, people are far less certain.

Many people who have been at the edge of death will tell what they saw. Some see what is going on around their clinically dead body. There are stories about that. A heart surgery patient sued a hospital because of self-reported harm suffered when the patient heard operating room staff ridiculing her obese body during bypass surgery. The patient told the court she knew exactly what the staff said because she was out of her body, watching and listening from above. She was unsuccessful in her suit and received no compensation.

Others see beyond that immediate "by-the-body" scene far into the world of death. And although people have different stories, their stories have common threads and themes: light and love, friends and family, heavenly beings and beauty. And, beyond what people who return from a near-death experience say they see and hear, there is a universal message they tell: Do not fear death. Death, near-death experiencers say, is not a void but a new and wondrous place from which they were snatched to return to earthly life.

Some near-death experiencers tell detailed stories. Others report mere glimpses of the other side. They draw pictures with consistent themes: their spirit floating near the ceiling, their body lying below, and workers scrambling to save them. Many find clear meaning in the death event. They share the reasons they were told to come back to earth, for example, to take care of children. Others do not know exactly why they are back; they were just told, "It's not your time." Each person passes into death with different eyes, but, through their stories, we can weave together a veritable picture of what life beyond death can be.

Near-death experiencers say the event has had a profound impact on how they lead their lives. The value they attach to personal relationships and work may change. Some go back to school or switch careers. Others move closer to family because they believe family ties are now more clear and mean-ingful. Many question what is important in their lives. The jour-ney beyond life changes many people. What to the observer is an outward experience, to the experiencer, often is an inward shuffling of perceptions and beliefs.

People who report near-death experiences reveal these com-monly occurring events:

- People move out of their bodies and, in spirit form, watch and hear the scene from a position above their bodies. This is sometimes called the "autoscopic" component.

- People feel relaxed and comfortable when outside their bodies. They feel no bodily pain.
- People travel through a tunnel toward a light.
- People journey far from the situation to beautiful, unearthly realms.
- People meet "higher, unearthly beings" and friends and relatives who have died before.
- People converse with their minds in dialogue that does not use words as we know them.
- People experience peacefulness beyond any known during life.
- People feel pulled back toward their bodies when they hear their names called.
- People are given a reason to return to life, given a choice to come back, or merely told, "It's not your time."
- People, upon return, feel they have experienced unconditional love, being accepted for who they are, and therefore they no longer fear death.
- People upon return may have discovered a purpose for their life unbeknownst to them before. They may choose to live their lives differently. Less annoyed by mundane problems, they focus more on spiritual awareness, connectedness, and service to fellow human beings and the universe.
- People have a hard time finding words to describe the breadth and depth and meaning of the near-death event.

Do Not Be Afraid

My role as a clinical nurse specialist in a large medical complex centered around helping people with loss. I often comforted patients and their families when death had struck unexpectedly or was insidiously moving closer. Because of my experience with death, I met Betty. Her story reveals commonly occurring components of a near-death event, i.e., the out-of-body experience, comfort, the tunnel, unearthly beings, acceptance of death as good, and the difficulty in communicating all this to other people.

It was no surprise when I was called to her room. At morning rounds, Betty told the resident doctor that the last time she had surgery, "I saw it all. I watched it from the ceiling." The resident shrugged off her comment in disbelief, but the nurse manager of the floor called me and said, "I think the patient is scared because the doctor did not believe she had an out-of-body experience during her previous surgery. Please come and talk to her."

Betty was so detailed in her story, I was amazed it had happened eight years before. She had been told by the nurse manager that I knew many people who had gone out of their bodies. Betty wondered if because she went out of her body during her last surgery, she might travel even further, closer to death. Would she die during her surgery today? If so, she wanted some time to say some good-byes. After assuring Betty that people may leave their bodies multiple times without dying, she began to tell her story.

Betty told me this: "I was scared to tell anyone about it. It was difficult to find words that described the experience and hard to get them out. And that is not because the experience was bad. No, it was good. It was the most quieting and relaxing experience I've ever had.

"It happened in surgery. One of the doctors who was here on rounds this morning was part of the surgical team then, too. I told him about this at my first postop check-up. He did not believe me then and does not believe me now. I asked him today if any other patient had told him a story like mine. He said emphatically, 'No.'

"Really, at first the words did not easily come out. I finally told my story to a doctor who was a social friend of mine. He said that a similar thing happened to his brother. I was relieved when the doctor believed me. This led me to start to talk to others. I told the chaplain and later the surgeon who operated on me.

"This is what happened. I had abdominal surgery that day. My son had just left my hospital room to go home. The nurse came in to take my blood pressure. I figured I was in trouble because the next thing I remember was watching the nurse push my bed out of the room. I was floating above the bed looking down. I could hear everything. She told other nurses I had no blood pressure. Doctors and nurses yelled orders at each other. I found myself going down a black tunnel. In the tunnel, I was being pushed on a cart by four people wearing gray tunics with hoods. Then I saw the light. The light made me feel safe . . . all right . . . safe.

"Then suddenly I was floating above everyone in the operating room. From above I watched my body as the anesthesiologist stuck a gray tube down my throat and put a mask over my face. The surgeon took out staples that he had put in earlier that day to close my stomach. He stopped my bleeding. I heard him call for blood. 'Call for some extra to be on hand. I know two people who have her type if need be. She's fifty-four years old, isn't she?' These words I clearly remember the doctor saying. As the surgeon finished, he patted me on the stomach. I thought that was rather an odd thing for a doctor to do.

"Only later did I get up the nerve to talk to my surgeon about all this. He believed me! He said I could never have known about him asking for extra blood, or talking about the two people he knew with my blood type, or that he patted my stomach, which he said he did remember doing.

"He added, however, that when I was wheeled into the operating room, he also said to me, 'Come back. You have to come back. You have kids to raise.' He said he patted my stomach at the end of the surgery as he told me to fight back and heal. The doctor told me later he tells all his patients this and hopes they can hear him somehow.

"I tell my children, 'Do not be afraid of death.' I learned it through this experience. I don't know why, but it was the main thought I had when I came back . . . that death is nothing to be afraid of."

Knowing people are not necessarily closer to a final death experience if they have out-of-body experiences during surgery helped Betty relax. Betty made it through surgery just fine. She did not report any details of this operation. She told me the last thing she recalled before awakening in the recovery room was the anesthesiologist talking to her as she went to sleep.

Tell Them about Him

I was one of four nurses working in the coronary care unit that evening. It was busy. We had two new admissions and one unstable patient named Carl. Beverly was Carl's nurse. In her change of shift report, she included a conversation that the patient had with God about returning to life.

Beverly said she shocked Carl with a cardiac defibrillator several times that shift. His heart rhythm kept going bad—ventricular tachycardia. He became unconscious. Beverly would hold the paddles on Carl's chest while the button for electrical current was pushed. The procedure would revive Carl.

After three or four such episodes within five hours, Carl asked Beverly to not shock him again. He said it was too painful and he didn't need it. Beverly told him that his heart needed to be shocked or it would beat too fast and he would die.

"But you don't understand," said Carl, "I will not die tonight. I have been to see God and God promised me I could return to teach my children about Him."

And Carl lived to do so.

Words Cannot Describe

Steve had lived and loved. He had experienced pain and illness. In fact, he thought he had seen the gamut life had to offer. But one day, October 26, 1990, he said he felt the ultimate in joy and peacefulness and he talked to God. According to Steve, his adventure into death began October 10th.

My chest hurt. I thought I pulled a muscle. I drove to the doctor's office where my electrocardiogram (EKG) showed otherwise. Paramedics transported me to the hospital emergency room where I was told my heart's electrical system had gone berserk.

The nurses hooked me up to all sorts of monitoring devices. Wires and tubes told them how I was doing. Suddenly my nurse told me she needed to transfer me into the ICU. By the time she pushed my bed halfway through the doorway, I had also started another journey unbeknownst to those frantically caring for me.

I felt much better than I had in years. I found myself floating as I entered heaven. It was so unbelievable . . . beautiful . . . words cannot describe the beauty I saw. There were people in the distance. Flowers bloomed everywhere in breathtaking colors. Yet there was a soft rosy hue that cast its shadow over everything.

I became aware of the presence of God. As He came closer to me, I felt all of His glory and power. But more than that, I sensed His love. Such love! He cradled me in all of His love. And then He spoke to me . . . mind to mind.

I cannot remember all that he said to me. But I distinctly remember my replies. I said first, "I'm dying?" Thoughts of my family instantly passed through my mind. God, knowing everything, was aware of my thoughts. God asked if I would like to stay.

I said to God, "It is so beautiful here and I love you my Lord and Savior." God replied that I had a choice to go back or to stay.

I said to God, "Lord, I now want to submit my will to yours. If you have some work for me to do, or my family needs me, then I am willing to go back. But the final decision is yours. I will do your will." After our discussion, the rosy hue faded.

Steve's journey beyond life ended. This near-death experience convinced him there was a life with God beyond death and God had plans for his life on earth. Steve prays daily for God to lead him to do His will. He believes God has a reason to send him back. He doesn't know the reason, but feels secure he will be led to do what is right.

Zapped

Listening has always been one of Anne's jobs. Before Anne was a nurse she was a hairdresser. Women talked to her about their health problems even when she was hairdresser.

Anne had been doing Leah's hair for years and really did not notice Leah's absence from her bookings until Leah came in apologizing for not making an appointment sooner. She explained that she had been in the hospital after suffering a heart attack. Leah's story did not end with a simple "I'm glad I survived." No, Anne emphasized, clients tell you their most intimate thoughts while they are in the chair. Leah was no exception. Leah told Anne this story about travel to an unearthly place where she met deceased family.

When my heart stopped, I left my body. I could see the doctor below and hear him say, "Leah, I'm going to zap you now. If you don't come back, I'll have to let you go." I saw everyone frantically working to revive me.

Suddenly, I found myself in a most beautiful place. My aunt and brother were there. I talked to them. They wanted me to come with them. I was happy, comfortable, really full of joy. But I felt that I had left something undone. I could not think of what it could be. But it was clear to me that I had to come back.

Then I was floating above again and I saw what they were doing as they took a machine and pressed metal paddles against my chest. My body jumped. I popped instantly back into my body. At the same time as I re-entered my body, I felt the most excruciating pain. My chest hurt.

Anne said Leah's story helped her understand death. Later, when, as a nurse, she witnessed a patient's clinical death, Anne knew, when others did not, that the patient was probably watching all the resuscitative measures being done. Afterward Anne was not afraid to talk to the patient about what she saw and heard while the patient's heart was stopped. Anne brought to her nursing practice what she had learned from Leah about her journey beyond life.

Now that Anne is an emergency room nurse, she has the opportunity to tell victims of accidents and sudden illnesses that it's all right to talk about how they felt when the emergency team worked on them. Some talk about watching from above the scene. Anne feels it's her responsibility to let patients know she's always there to listen.

It's Not Your Time

I recently took care of an eighteen year old accident victim named Bill. He had crashed while driving a motorcycle and one of his legs became amputated upon impact. Blood loss caused the young man to have cardiorespiratory failure. He stopped breathing. Then his heart stopped. Bill shared with me what happened. He told me that his beliefs and values were altered by this near-death event. A changed young man emerged.

Bill said, "Time seemed to speed up. I felt like everything was all right, even though I sure wasn't. I was bleeding to death and yet I felt at peace, united with all the world. I wasn't even afraid. I could see my leg was gone but I didn't feel any pain. I could see a lot of blood but I was calm and comfortable. There was this incredible peacefulness that came out of nowhere."

Then Bill saw someone that he called "the Lord." He said God talked kindly to him. Bill said God told him "It is not your time." Shortly thereafter, Bill felt himself pop suddenly back in his body. He was revived by emergency workers.

Bill told me he has not figured out why he went beyond life and back. The accident has changed his life in many ways. He will be in therapy for a long time. He cannot go back to the construction job he had before. He is considering returning to school. What he will do with his life Bill does not know. He does feel he is destined to do something different. Bill will definitely pursue a career of service to others rather than just a well-paying job. Bill says this near-death experience changed his life. He looks at life with a new reverence. Bill feels his experience in death has made him want to be a better person, not just to live through an eight-hour workday but to reach out and give to others.

She Felt Honored

Deb is a nurse on a hospice unit where patients with cancer often stay until they die. Deb hesitated before she told me she felt honored that a patient would share the following story with her. "It isn't the sort of thing you would tell just anyone," she commented. But knowing Deb as I do, I can easily understand why the patient's chose to open up to her. Deb is a good listener, and she always tries to understand.

Deb met Margaret during one of the patient's hospitalizations for cancer. Margaret's condition had been labeled terminal. At one point in her illness, before Margaret knew Deb, Margaret was comatose. Deb asked Margaret about this lapse of consciousness, how long it had lasted and when it had occurred.

Margaret told Deb that while in the coma, she remembered clearly floating off to have a "glimpse of heaven." She described heaven as a beautiful place—one which human words cannot begin to describe. She wanted to stay but knew she had to return.

While lapsing in and out of consciousness, Margaret said she floated above her body lying in the hospital bed. She also saw and heard the family that had gathered around her bed. When she recovered from the coma, she told her family that she had been out of her body looking down seeing and hearing them. They laughed and said she must have been dreaming or hallucinating because she was on strong medicines for pain. They did not believe her.

At least they did not believe her until she told the group what she had heard them discussing. Margaret saw members of her family and heard them plan her funeral. She told them in detail how they disagreed about the church and about the catering expense. Margaret was able to quote word for word, to an embarrassed group, the conversations family members had at her bedside.

Margaret was not mad at her family. Like so many people who cross over to the other side and come back, she thought there were more important issues to think about than these people's insensitivity. Margaret guessed they would be more sensitive once she shared her out-of-body and near-death experience with them. She felt it was very important that she tell her family and her nurse, Deb, about life beyond death.

What was Deb's reaction to her patient's revelations? She told me: "This experience has changed me in ways I am still not fully aware of. I believe there are other people like Margaret who may see when their eyes are not open and may hear when their family thinks they do not. I tell families that a person is a body and a spirit. And, when critically ill, some people leave their bodies and float in spirit form looking down at the people below. I often think of Margaret and how convinced she was that there is existence beyond this life. I talk to patients in comas, now. They may hear me."

Successive, Successful Revivals

I've been asked whether people who attempt suicide are welcomed into life after death. I would say, "yes." My sources of information are my own experience and the research of Dr. Bruce Greyson. Greyson's research (1986) shows that many suicide attempters have near-death experiences. Such experiences may strengthen their ability to face life's demands later. This story comes from Mark, a patient I cared for in an ICU. During cardiopulmonary arrest, he met, in a light at the end of the tunnel, a brother who had committed suicide.

Mark has had several cardiac arrests due to heart attacks and heart failure. He remembers well his experiences in emergency rooms when hospital staff scrambled to save him. Mark reported to me that, on more than one occasion, he found himself floating above the table his body was on as emergency personnel tried to revive him. He watched. He heard. He saw everything, even when an incision was made in his chest to place a pacemaker. He felt no pain.

During these arrest episodes, Mark felt himself going out through the corner of the room and then traveling through a long tunnel. He moved toward a very bright light. Once he entered the light, he saw his parents, long dead, and his brother who had committed suicide, coming toward him. Their hands were outstretched toward him in greeting. Mark felt warmly welcomed.

But Mark returned to the emergency room scene and, after floating above the scene again, popped back into his body. He tells people he does not know why he survived to tell about this journey.

See You Later

Do children have near-death experiences? Yes. And their accounts can be clear with details describing an event much like adults encounter. Erin was a little girl whose family were my friends. When

I listened to her, I heard about heaven. She was just eleven years-old when she had a near-death event.

Erin's family moved to our city hoping that the high-tech university hospital could cure her cancer. She was vibrant, brave, and hopeful. She swam. She went to movies. She ate pizza. She giggled when talking about boys. She enjoyed all the things young girls do.

Although the most modern treatments were tried, Erin's condition worsened. She became tired and uncomfortable. She was a prisoner, so to speak, in the pediatric intensive care unit, for fear she would get an infection if she ventured out where people could infect her with a cold or flu. Life now for Erin, as she lay in her protective isolation cubicle, was a series of visits from doctors and nurses to check her medical status, from technicians who took her blood or X-rayed her body, and from those closest to her—immediate family and her pastor.

One spring day at 2 p.m. Erin's friend, Ellen, age ten, gowned, masked, and gloved to protect Erin from germs, entered Erin's cubicle. I heard the girls joke about how Ellen looked—gown down to the floor, glasses barely peeking over the mask, gloves with fingers hanging limp at the ends because they were much too long.

They talked about their brothers and the trouble they were always getting into. Ellen told Erin the boys had just made a huge fort on a hill outside the houses. It collapsed on top of them and they had to scramble for their lives. Ellen and Erin laughed. I had to reposition Erin's oxygen mask because of their boistrous activity.

Then Erin got serious. She told Ellen, as I stood near, "You know I've been through a tunnel and I sat on Jesus's lap. He told me not to be afraid. He was just like Pastor Dean said He is. Jesus was so nice. He said I can go be with him. I want to go. I am tired."

Erin said dying—when she visited Jesus—felt good. She said she would be leaving to go back to heaven soon. She wanted to say good-bye to everyone and let them know she would be with Jesus. Ellen went home at 3:30 p.m. Erin died at 9:00 p.m.

I still am moved by the clear and explicit words of this child. I shared what Erin told Ellen with the family that they might find the peace this child conveyed she felt when she journeyed beyond life.

Going toward the Voice

One of my friends, Ellen, a CCU nurse, worked right up until her child's expected date of arrival. Her supervisor told her she should not do CPR that night or there would be both a code and a delivery in the same room. But as Ellen looked back on that evening, she was very glad she had been there. She shared this near-death experience in which a patient felt compelled to return to his body when hearing his name called. Ellen was Charlie's assigned nurse for the shift. This was her fifth straight evening of caring for him. He was in unstable condition.

When Charlie's heart went into ventricular tachycardia, Ellen apologized to him while at the same time delivering a hard thump with her fist to his chest and pleading, "Charlie, come back!" Hitting the chest of a patient whose heartbeat has gone haywire sometimes jolts the heart back to a good rhythm.

But Charlie's heart rhythm did not change. This was what we call a code situation. Ellen began CPR. Others came running into CCU and gave Charlie drugs and used electric paddles to change his heart rhythm to one that worked.

Ellen talked to Charlie after he was stable. He told her he felt his spirit lift from the bed just before her fist made contact with chest. Charlie did not feel the blow to his chest. He said he was not feeling any pain when he "floated" above the resuscitation scene. He said he could see his body on the bed but felt himself—the real core of Charlie—above, looking down at all that was happening.

Charlie said he heard Ellen calling him back and was drawn to her voice. He kept trying to get closer to Ellen's voice until, unexpectedly, he found himself popped back into his body. Charlie said one moment he was viewing all that was happening from a comfortable position above the scene and then, all of a sudden, he was back in his body looking up at staff's faces and, for the first time, feeling pain in his chest.

Ellen was stunned when Charlie told her his story. She became convinced she was meant to be there that night. It made the new life that she carried—born two days later—even more special.

Now Ellen is very conscientious about what she says around patients who are critically ill. She talks directly to them. She calls each by name. In a code situation, she tells the person to come back. She tells patients she is trying to get them back. I believe patients may hear Ellen and be drawn to her voice like Charlie was.

Doctors May Not Be the Closest Ones to God

After I addressed a group of emergency room doctors and nurses, a man approached me in the conference center lobby. He introduced himself as an internal medicine physician. He said he came to my talk on death and dying because he wanted to know if other people experienced events similar to what he had while undergoing CPR. This doctor described a classic near-death event. He emphasized a peacefulness he found incredible. He later wrote to tell me how my talk about death validated his experience and changed his medical practice. He also sent along a picture he drew of his body in an ICU bed and his spirit hovering in a corner above the crowd of health-care workers at his bedside. What follows are the doctor's words.

I was admitted to the intensive care unit because I had chest pain. All the tests and therapies I had learned in medical school, on my way to becoming a doctor, were now being performed on me. I was a doctor and now became a patient.

Just like other patients whose hearts stopped, I was suddenly surrounded by a CPR team. This is when I felt myself rise out of my body. I was going out . . . but my body lay behind . . . and my spirit was leaving out of the corner of the room into the open sky.

A spirit—this they didn't tell me about in medical school or in my practice as a doctor in a big hospital. No one ever talked during CPR about the person whose body we were working on. We talked bodies. We talked about CPR measures. We discussed facts like heart rate, rhythm, blood pressure. We barked out orders. I don't recall any doctor I worked with ever mentioning a patient by first name during CPR.

When I was out of my body and, as a spirit, watching from a place near the ceiling as the medical staff performed CPR on me I did not see a tunnel. But there was an open, peaceful sky. The sky shown brightly . . . radiantly. There was incredible calmness all around. And I was comfortable. Peacefulness, like I never experienced before, overtook me. I felt united with God.

During this CPR episode, when my spirit floated above my body, part of my head was outside and part of my head was still in the room. I was about to go out through the corner of the room when my wife called my name. I looked back down and, when I saw her, and heard her plead my name again and again, I felt a tremendous pull. I instantly returned to my body.

Since this event, I feel that the life I am living is a gift. I believe that at that particular moment—when I was about to leave the room—if my wife had not called me, I would not have returned. I sensed immediately that I am supposed to do something more for others in this life.

In addition to this lesson, I learned that my patients may be watching me from a position above . . . near God . . . when I do emergency procedures on them. What a joke . . . patients think we doctors are the ones close to God. I learned that a patient may be very close to God, especially when that person is in very critical condition.

Angel In Blue

This story was told to me by a middle-aged woman who faces the eventuality of death each day. She had spent many days at a hospital when her child received treatment for cancer. The woman is not the only person to describe to me angels who wear blue, flowing gowns. This is Jodie's mom's story. Her belief in angels comforts her.

I wasn't Carrie's mother. I am Jodie's mom. Jodie, like Carrie, was hospitalized in a children's hospital. Carrie's mother couldn't visit because she was a single parent struggling to support her four kids. It was difficult for her to visit Carrie and also care for the three younger children at home while working two jobs.

So Carrie was in the hospital without family while dying of cancer. And you could tell the whole medical staff made a point of spending as much time as possible with her. They played games with her. They brought her home-baked cookies. The nurses gave her special assignments "to help them." So Carrie was kept busy.

There were times, though, when Carrie seemed very alone and frightened. She would pace the floor for hours, her head bowed down, her arms bent in as if to make a protective shell around her. It was at these times, more than once, her unhappy expression briefly met my eyes and then quickly lowered again toward the floor. I looked at her and felt the sadness within her.

One night when Carrie and my daughter played checkers, Carrie told us a story. She said a woman from heaven came to visit her in the hospital.

Carrie said a beautiful angel-like person wearing a soft blue gown came down a winding stairway in the corner of her room. The woman told Carrie that things would be all right. Carrie said she felt good when the "angel in blue" visited.

After the "angel in blue" visited Carrie, I did notice a change in her. I could see she was less agitated after this experience of meeting the angel from heaven. Carrie no longer paced the halls alone. She was calmer. She went out, and, with eyes making contact, talked to people. This calming presence that coincided with Carrie seeing the angel stayed with the child through her death a few days later.

There was no winding stairway in Carrie's room. It was a regular hospital room. But I believe someone came to visit and console Carrie. And I am convinced that the woman from another world was destined to comfort this child. And so it appeared.

Was there a reason my daughter was hospitalized at the same time as Carrie? I have often wondered if it was to let me know that comforting angels are there to help children when they die.

Listening Ears

Nurses who come to my talks on recognition and response to near-death experiences want to know what to say to a patient who has a near-death event. I tell them that patients need listening ears more than any therapeutic talk when they begin to share what has happened. The opportunity to be heard is not always there for people. Witness Natalie's story about her husband's near-death event.

Natalie had been a nurse fifteen years when her husband, Colin, experienced a near-death event. Colin had emergency surgery for injuries he received in a motor vehicle accident. Afterward he remarked to Natalie that, during the surgery, he floated outside of his body looking down at the operating room staff and himself on the table. Natalie dismissed this tale of Colin's as an anesthesia-related hallucination. She had not heard of out-of-body experiences. She cut Colin short when he attempted to talk of it.

Twelve years later, Natalie attended one of my presentations at the hospital where she works as an RN. The focus was on interventions professional nurses could use to support patients who had near-death events. She came home, put the materials she received on the kitchen counter, and began to prepare dinner.

Colin came home and pulled a chair up in the kitchen. He looked over the true-and-false test lying on the counter. Natalie had taken the pretest before the lecture to measure her knowledge of near-death events. "Guess you don't know as much as I do about all this," Colin said when he saw her low score. He paced back and forth in the kitchen, test in hand.

Natalie returned a puzzled look to Colin. Colin seized the opportunity to talk. He spilled out the details of his experience, after the car crash twelve years earlier, just before he was wheeled to the operating room. He could remember clearly how everything looked.

He recalled how Natalie stood by the cart as doctors explained what they needed to do in emergency surgery and got her consent. He described the green surgical sheet that covered his body. Colin went on to tell Natalie he felt his spirit move like a shadow to a position above and to one side of the body—his own—that he saw still lying on the cart. He said he felt himself floating at ceiling height in the corner of the room. He remembered he saw Natalie and the doctors below.

Since Natalie was now listening, with attentive ears and mind, Colin continued to give an account of a bright light—"brighter than a halogen lamp"—yet not annoying to him. He said he entered a long tunnel. He remembered experiencing a feeling of great joy and peace. He knew he was without fear. Then, he said, his "shadow spirit" popped back into his body.

"You were right there, Natalie," reminded Colin, "but you didn't know where I really was."

Natalie now listened without interrupting. She believed Colin and told him so. She described to him near-death experiences she had heard about in class. Colin always knew what had happened to him was real. But no one had really heard him before. Natalie's increased knowledge of near-death events opened her mind and ears to Colin's experience.

Revolution

Dan, a paramedic, often responds to motor vehicle accident scenes. Some victims make it. Some never leave the pavement, or so Dan thought until he talked to a victim afterward. Dan's story describes how many emergency personnel have come to believe that accident victims leave their bodies, feel no pain, and watch the scene from above.

Stacey was a patient Dan helped remove from a five car pileup. At the scene, she was motionless and unresponsive. The Jaws of Life had to be used to break the car apart and get her out. Dan said to himself, "This one's not going anywhere for a long time." He helped get Stacey onto a backboard and into the ambulance. Stacey then started to moan.

It was rare that Dan ever talked to anyone he rescued after an emergency. But his mother, a teacher, asked him to look in on Stacey, who was a former student of hers. A few weeks later, when Dan arrived early at the hospital for a class, he went to Stacey's room.

Dan introduced himself to Stacey. He said he was sorry for any pain he had to put her through to get her out of the wrecked car. Dan judged that Stacey, suffering a broken collarbone, shattered arm, broken legs, and multiple cuts and bruises, was trapped, cramped up in a tiny space between the seat and the dashboard, for one and a half hours. Dan was taken aback when Stacey said she felt nothing until her body was placed on the board. Stacey later told Dan she left her body behind when the cars collided. Floating above, in no pain and with clear thought, she said she counted the revolutions the car made as it rolled down the embankment. Stacey told Dan which areas of glass on the car broke with each revolution. She said she saw her body in the car as it rolled.

From the way she was pinned and her neck immobilized, Dan knew that Stacey couldn't have seen all the damage the car sustained, much less, in her condition, be able to know specifically when each section of glass had shattered. That is, not unless, as she said, she wasn't in her body at the time but was at a vantage point to observe the accident.

At accidents, Dan now wonders if the person he is helping is watching him work. Usually the victims are not able to talk to him, so he doesn't know for sure. But Dan believes it is possible.

She Always Rocked . . . Even When She Met Me

Most people think that when someone dies they won't ever see that person again—at least in their own lifetime. Laura was 47 years old when she discovered otherwise. An aunt she had been close to met her in the tunnel during the near-death experience she describes. Laura's account contains an out-of-body journey through a tunnel. At the end of the tunnel there is light and the message that she must return.

Laura thought she had seen Aunt Vi for the last time at her funeral. Laura was the one who read the eulogy from the nieces and nephews because she was the oldest. In fact, she was the one who probably knew Aunt Vi best because she was given the duty of cleaning her house.

This was 1935. When your parents told you to go clean your aunt's house, you did. Being the oldest of seven kids whose ages ranged from 17 to 3l, Laura had a lot of jobs to do. Every week it was the same. Get the bucket of cleaning supplies—ammonia, rags, furniture polish. Cross the street and say hello to Aunt Vi who was always rocking away on the front porch. She had a shawl. Laura used to straighten it as she passed her. Nothing much was said. Laura never could say what she really felt about this cleaning job. She kept her thoughts to herself.

This was unpaid work done out of family obligations, family pride, and duty to one's elders. Laura also cleaned other places. For these she got paid. In addition, she got to see how other people live—closets full of fashionable clothes, pictures, vases of flowers. Those houses were more fun to clean because all the things Laura saw were new, different, and interesting.

But working at Aunt Vi's place was a family responsibility for Laura. Aunt Vi became a regular part of her life. It had been thirty years since her death until Laura saw her again.

Ulcers appear in Laura's family like mold on tomatoes after a heavy rainy season. Her dad had a bad stomach. Laura had part of her stomach removed but still suffered, at 47, from periods of intense pain.

On this night, Laura was in so much pain she couldn't get off the floor. She just lay there. Everything hurt too much to move. Her husband was panic-stricken. What could he do? The ambulance people he called loaded her on board and soon she was in the operating room of a nearby hospital.

Laura remembers seeing and hearing people she didn't know yelling her last name, age, and orders for this and that. She recalls seeing workers dressed in green hospital suits. She said she watched the operating room scene from a place above. She looked down at her body that lay on a table as the doctors cut into her. But she didn't feel the knife blade at all. Laura suddenly realized that she was out of her body.

Two doctors and two nurses were around the table. "She'll never make it," one doctor said. The other doctor just looked up over his mask and then back down at his hands that were feverishly cutting through layers. Laura floated further and left the operating room.

Laura remembers clearly going through the tunnel and seeing the light at the end. Nothing was bothering her. She felt good. She did not feel any pain. She was not scared. She was at peace. There at the end of the tunnel of light sat her Aunt Vi. She was on her rocker still, looking just as she had when Laura came over to clean. "Go back, my dear," were her words to Laura. "Go back, my dear."

Who knows how long Laura was in the tunnel?. She doesn't. She doesn't know why her aunt was there. Aunt Vi didn't look like an angel or anything heavenly. No, she looked like she needed her shawl straightened back on her shoulder, just like years ago.

By the time she got back to the operating room from the tunnel, the doctors had removed most of Laura's stomach. Her colon would thereafter serve to digest her food. From a position right above them, Laura looked down and she could see they were sewing her up. The doctors looked tired, really drained. They told her husband that they had to restart her heart two times.

Laura knows that one doctor could have given up when the other said she couldn't be saved. She's been back in life for 25 years now. Laura now know what happens when you die. You keep living. To the Doc who wouldn't give up, she says "Thanks." She always remembers him in her prayers.

The Ride

The nurse who tells this story came forth because she hopes the lesson she learned will help others. Dora had been a nurse only three years when Jerry, a critically ill man, revealed his near-death experience to her. She did not believe him then. Now she does. This story reminds health care workers that the critically ill may be watching what the workers do, and hearing what they say.

I was Jerry's nurse in the intensive care unit. I was here when they brought him in from the local hospital to which he was first taken after he collapsed at home. His condition was critical. His heart had stopped at home and twice during the transport. We all felt he was a lucky man to have survived three cardiac arrests in two hours. Now we were treating him with multiple drugs, and watching and waiting.

I was kind of surprised when Jerry said, "My daughter told me that they helicoptered me from the local hospital to this medical center when my heart stopped for the second time in a half hour. She is frightened that I'll die. I don't blame her. She was crying when they put me on the cart and rushed me past her into the hall and out to the waiting chopper. I know I saw her sobbing. She doesn't need to worry. I'm sticking around." Most of the patients I had cared for in the three months I had been a cardiac ICU nurse were not so confident, especially when even we staff members believed it was a moment-by-moment waiting game to see what would happen.

Then Jerry told me about the helicopter ride. He said he remembers the paramedics pushing the cart with his body on it down the hospital corridor. He said he was floating above the cart in a position near the ceiling. He said that the part of him that was looking down at his body on the cart kept pace with the movement of people rushing toward the helicopter pad. Jerry said he was drawn to his daughter's crying, but, on the whole, he felt peaceful. He was not afraid.

Jerry was fully aware of his heart stopping a third time when the copter was airborne. Again he watched the medics as they slapped the metal paddles on his chest and pressed the button to send an electrical charge through his body. He saw his body lift slightly off the cart when the charge was delivered. But Jerry felt nothing, no pain. And then he left the helicopter scene and found himself being propelled down a long tunnel. Jerry said he had no control over where he was going. He was traveling as if magnetized by some unseen force.

As Jerry went through the tunnel, he said he began to feel bathed in warmth from a light. He felt good. He wasn't worried about the body he had left behind. Suddenly Jerry saw his cousin Joyce, who had died ten years before. She had always been one of his favorite relatives. In fact, if he had to name his closest relative as he grew up, it would have been Joyce. Jerry told me Joyce said, "It's not your time, Jerry. You need to go back." He said she said those same words twice.

Jerry found himself pulled back into his body while on the helicopter. Then he felt his chest hurt. He moaned in pain. Jerry wanted to tell his daughter about seeing Joyce and the message she had given him. He asked me if I would be there with him while he told her. He said he didn't want her to think he concocted this story because of the drugs he was being given for pain or because he had "gone crazy" due to his heart stopping so many times.

I wish I could tell you that I said, "Sure, Jerry, I'll be there and help you tell her." But I did not. This was the first time I had heard about a journey beyond life. I told him I had to go admit a new patient.

It was only a year or so later, after I had heard more patients tell stories like Jerry's, that I became convinced that something—the same thing—must have happened to many patients during CPR. I have often thought of Jerry. I wonder if he ever told his daughter. I did not believe him. I did not help him. I was so brusque. Did he know that I didn't believe then what I now know to be true?

I have learned that the most critical part of good communication is listening. I listen to what my patients say about going out of their bodies. They tell me that they were unafraid during their out-of-body journey but they are now scared to tell other people. They are afraid people will think they are crazy. I wish I could go back in time and help the patients whose stories I disregarded. I tell new nurses to listen to patients' stories about where they were when their hearts stopped. I tell nurses I believe that patients experiencing clinical death can journey beyond life and, later, return. I tell new nurses I believe that patients can journey beyond life and return.

I Need to Know

When tragedy strikes, nurses are often the people who help families communicate their feelings and their fears to one another. Family members, many times, become closer when they face illness or accidents together. Claudia, a trauma life support nurse, tells this story. It starts when Kris, hospitalized with multiple severe injuries, wanted to know what death was like for her infant daughter.

Kris, a young mother, had lost her baby. Sara, the infant, was born alive but died a short few months after, the tragic victim of a car getting out of control and hitting a crowd of pedestrians on the sidewalk. Kris played the picture of the accident over and over in her mind. A sunny day, the stroller being torn from her hands, the overpowering sound of the vehicle as it ripped her baby from her grasp, her screams for help, the pain of her own injury that made her unable to move to look for her daughter—it all went so quickly. She asked for Sara. Where was Sara? She remembers being in the emergency room when her husband told her that Sara was struck by the car and died.

Now, two days later, she asks herself the same questions over and over. What could she have done differently? Why did this happen? What had she done wrong? Where was her baby? What did Sara feel when she was hit? Did she suffer? The doctors told Kris and her husband that Sara had died upon impact when the car pushed her stroller into a the wall of a building.

When Claudia was helping Kris with her morning cares, a bath in bed, because of the IVs running and casts on her arms and one leg, Kris looked up and said, "My mother had a near-death experience when I was born. She says she never wants to talk about it. I need to know about it. Now that my baby has died I want to know what mother saw. It is important. I want to know what death is like, what my little Sara went through. How can I get mother to tell me?"

Claudia could tell that knowing about the dying process meant a lot to Kris. Kris paid no attention to the chit-chat Claudia interjected as she carried out the bath. In fact, Kris's voice was pleading. She wanted to know what death was like. Claudia said she'd try to talk to Kris's mother next time she came to visit.

After the accident, Kris's mother tried very hard to keep up a cheery front for the sake of her daughter. She brought in home-made soup and bread to try to hearten Kris. Claudia helped Kris's mom take the food she brought to the unit's refrigerator. She took this opportunity to open conversation about death. Claudia said, "Kris told me that you nearly died when she was born. She said you had a near-death experience."

Kris's mother appeared startled that Claudia knew. But she did not back off. "Yes, I believe I did. Do you believe I could have?" Claudia asked Kris's mother to tell her what happened.

For Kris's mother the details remained clear, although the event occurred 27 years before. She started her story by telling of the people who would not talk with her about it— her doctor and the nurse who was in the delivery room. "I never wanted to tell Krissy about it because the doctor and nurse said to not talk about it. The nurse said I would be crazy to want to talk about it. I didn't want my daughter to think I was crazy. It just slipped out that I told Krissy I had a near-death experience when she was born. I mentioned it to her after I had watched a

TV program about near-death. In fact the only people I've been able to tell about it all these years are the people who talk about it on TV. I find that when they tell about their experiences, I start talking right aloud to the TV. I find I'm saying, "Sure, that happened to me, too. I didn't want to come back. I was so comfortable even though I knew it was a hard delivery and I could see the doctor and nurse pushing on my stomach. I saw that light. It was beautiful. I wanted to stay but I was told to come back to take care of Krissy and her sister."

Kris's mother then looked up at Claudia and said "I believe I had a near-death experience. When Helen Jones, the nurse who was in the delivery room when Krissy was born, retired, she came into my store. I was still curious about the event, so I went over and I asked her if she remembered what happened to me when Krissy was born. She was a big, old nurse, gruff but nice. She said she didn't want to talk about it and I shouldn't either. "You have a good, healthy baby and you are all right. That's all that matters now," she said. And she turned and walked out.

"Do you believe me?" Kris's mother asked.

"Yes," Claudia responded, "I believe you. And, further, I believe that what you saw when you nearly died may help Kris now deal with the death of Sara. She wants to know if Sara is all right. Can you tell her that you were comfortable and what the place was like where you found yourself?"

Kris's mother agreed to talk to Kris about the near-death experience if Claudia would agree to be present. Kris listened to her mother's story without interrupting. Her mother told about beautiful gardens and music. She said she felt no pain and, in fact, felt so good she wanted to stay and not return to life. She said her aunt and a brother who had died before greeted her.

"Do you think Grandma Janet was there to welcome Sara?" asked Kris.

"Probably Grandpa Russell, too," said her mom.

Kris said that thinking Sara could be with her grandparents was comforting. She had such good times with them. Kris pressed her mom on the fact that she was comfortable and felt no pain even though she was in childbirth. Kris said she wanted to think that Sara felt no pain at the accident scene and that Sara quickly passed over into death.

When Claudia left Kris's room, she knew Kris had a better picture of what had happened to her baby. Kris was calmed and her mother was relieved of the burden not to tell. Claudia's belief that near-death events can be comforting to the grieving helped this family in their difficulty.

Readied to Come Back and Help

There was only a two-week span between the time of Ed's near-death experience and his death. But the interval was purposeful. Lynette, Ed's wife of two years, tells this story. She said that Ed asked her to write down what he saw and how he felt when his heart stopped. Someday, Lynette said, she will share Ed's story with his son. This story illustrates how a person's feelings and way of being with others may change after experiencing the unconditional love present in a near-death event.

Ed was not happy with his son, Jamie. Jamie was what Ed called a junkie—a 19-year-old high school dropout who sold drugs to middle- and high-school kids. There was considerable tension between father and son. Ed's first heart attack occurred right on the heels of an accusatory argument and fistfight with Jamie. Ed collapsed in pain at home. Lynette called an ambulance which rushed him to the emergency room.

While in the hospital, Ed's heart stopped. He floated above his body during CPR. He noticed that suddenly the pain in his chest and arm was gone. From a corner of the room, he could see doctors and nurses working over his body that lay in the bed. Four "angels"—two at his head and two at his feet—

escorted him out of the corner of the room. As his spirit left, the shouting of the emergency crew was dampened and then overtaken by extraordinarily melodious music. Ed said this music was more beautiful than any he had ever heard. Soon Ed was on his way through a tunnel and into a bright light. Describing the bright light was difficult for Ed. He said that if you piled all the precious gems into a heap and shined bright lights upon the pile, you would have only a vague sense of the extreme brightness. Ed said that the colors he experienced were more intense than he had ever seen before. He told of a banquet room filled with many loving souls dressed in white and gold.

But what affected Ed most was the immense love and forgiveness that radiated all around the environment. He felt loved. He saw his life reviewed in terms of how his actions affected other people. He said it was as though he was being asked to judge himself.

It scared Jamie to see his father get angry and collapse in front of him in the kitchen. He feared that he had caused the heart attack. When he visited Ed in the hospital, the two had a long talk, a talk about subjects long overdue being discussed.

Although he did not tell Jamie of the near-death event, Ed was able to identify and communicate how concerned he was for his son because he loved him. He had always yelled at Jamie, "I'm your father. I know more than any young kid, so listen to me." This time he asked Jamie to listen to him because he loved him and cared about what happened to him. Ed found he could be loving and non-judgmental. Jamie responded to his father's outpouring of love. He entered a drug treatment program a week before his father's second heart attack and death.

People say they learn something about themselves and their relationships to others by experiencing death. Some are lucky enough to be able to use what they learn.

The Funnel Force

This story was told to me forty years after it happened. The story-teller is Lydia, a woman who attended a university lecture I gave. Very often people come up to me after I have explained the characteristics of a near-death event and they exclaim, "I've had one!" Lydia's near-death event, however, was not comforting like most other people's I've heard but, as she said, "terrifying."

Lydia was only ten years old when she felt death approaching but she said she recalled the experience with such detail one would believe it had happened the same day she revealed it to me. Here is what occurred.

I could feel my fever getting higher as the day became night. I also sensed my parents were becoming increasingly anxious. My mother was usually the calm one. My dad was nervous and remote by nature. He paced outside the bedroom door. They had called a doctor to make a house call, believing I might have a contagious disease. My parents had already lost my older brother to polio.

I remember feeling very small as I lay in my parents double bed. I picked, in a monotonous rhythm, at the wallpaper most of the day. Suddenly I felt compelled to look up at the corner of the room opposite the big bed where I was.

I was drawn to that corner where a dark funnel-like tunnel opened up before me. I was very, very frightened when a force I could not resist pulled me into the funnel. I tried to pull back. I could not. I was pulled into the dark vortex.

The next thing I recall was sitting up in bed, hugging my father, which otherwise never happened, and screaming. I really couldn't find words to explain what had happened and scared me so. I could not describe it until I heard you talk about the tunnel. I think I must have just started down it when I was pulled back into my body. I clung to my father that day until I was asleep.

Please Don't Let That Happen Again

Carolyn worked as an ICU nurse for the past five years. She had heard several patients' stories of their experience in clinical death (no heart beat, no breathing) during CPR. Patients told her they felt renewed and very loved by the event. That is, all except Marilyn, who anxiously fought off feelings of fear and helplessness after experiencing a near-death event. This is a patient's account of what happened when her heart and breathing stopped. This near-death experience was distressing.

I know I clutched Carolyn's arm with a snapping turtle grip. I couldn't let go. Carolyn looked at me and told me I was all right. She said, "We needed to do CPR on you. You are back with us now in intensive care. You are okay, Marilyn."

Then the emergency team began to leave my bedside. There were staff talking about the details of what had happened, and there was the clanking of carts as machines were rolled back to their appointed places in the ICU. I was scared they'd leave me alone. I pulled harder on Carolyn's arm and begged, "Please, don't let this happen to me again."

Carolyn stayed at my side. She gently touched my body, helping me into a comfortable position. She offered to give me a backrub. I said "yes" because I desperately wanted Carolyn to stay. I was so very frightened. I wanted someone with me.

Minutes before I had watched from a place in the upper corner of the room as Carolyn did CPR. It hurt when a lot when Carolyn first started to pound on my chest but, seconds later, when I left my body, I felt no pain. I watched from a spot at the ceiling as the other ICU personnel ran over to help Carolyn.

All of a sudden I found myself in a "place of emptiness." There was no tunnel, no light, no beautiful music or scenery that others say they see when they have had CPR. Everything appeared a colorless gray. It was dark and I felt very, very alone in the midst of it.

I heard my deceased husband, Mel, call out my name. His voice was distorted and he sounded as though he was in a lot of pain. I continued to be scared.

Stranded and alone, that's how I felt. Then I popped back into my body and again felt the excruciating pain in my chest. I am not of any religious faith. I am not close to God. When Carolyn asked me, I had to tell her I did not experience a life review during this time. I still am anxious. I awake during the night thinking I hear Mel's voice. I wonder if I should go to church. I don't know what this experience all means, but something is not right.

There Is a Pond
My friend recalls the coolness of the blue-brown water
and the stillness of the water lilies that lay upon it.
I remember the vibrant, blowing, bent over, green marsh grass
and the clusters of black-eyed susans leading to the shore.
A boy looks at the pond
and sees a large-mouth bass
hooked on the end of his line.
We each view the pond with different eyes.
We see what is important to each one of us.
So we each view life and death with our own eyes.

There is a pond.

CHAPTER FIVE

If I Should Die . . . Let Me Go

Now I lay me
down to sleep
I pray the Lord
my soul to keep.
If I should die
before I wake,
I pray the Lord
my soul to take.

This children's prayer is repeated ritually by millions every night. Many people really desire what it pleads— to let their soul travel—be taken by God—when they die. Some are able to tell family, friends, and health-care professionals that this is their conscious choice.

You see, not everyone wants to be pulled back into this life after journeying beyond. But what enables some to stay in the unearthly realm, and others to return to this existence, we do not know. When you listen to people's stories, you may conclude that the timing of death may have some connection with intent, faith, willpower, and deep desire.

To know one wants to die comes in varied ways for people. Sometimes a person, exhausted by the ravages of illness, seeks to leave this earth because the person cannot tolerate any more pain. The person may enter a health-care facility where comfort, not further treatment, is provided.

Others may learn through an episode of near-death that they want to stay on the other side after, perhaps, completing a few tasks here. After experiencing a near-death event, a patient may adamantly say, "Let me go next time."

It's often hard to tell loved ones of the decision to leave. Some people make many trips back and forth before telling family to let them go. People who are leaving may gradually disengage from conversation with family, friends, and health care workers. I've learned this through watching and listening. Then these people often plead, "I do not want your pills. I want to go. I'm ready. Do not call me back."

Also there are those people who never tell family or friends they are choosing to go. They may die when family members are not present. They may pass on just when family members break vigil to go out for a meal. These people, it seems, choose to spare their loved ones looking at the actual death.

Others seek to be surrounded by those family and friends whom they've told they are dying. These people may ask that their hands be held or their heads stroked as one does to a child with a fever. And some desperately cry for anyone—such as a paramedic they do not know—to be with them as they cross over.

As I have observed patients die, I noted some patterns that influence how, when, and why they let go:

- Letting go may be rooted in a longing to be freed from physical or emotional pain.

- Letting go may gain headway after a person experiences freedom from bodily discomfort and unconditional love during a near-death event.
- Letting go may be based in a fervent desire to be with a loved one who has gone before.
- Letting go may rest on the belief that one's purpose on earth has been fulfilled and the other world is calling.
- Letting go may happen when the dying person knows family are ready to accept death and/or have support people around to help when death occurs.
- Letting go may be influenced by family, friends, or health-care professionals giving the dying person permission to pass on.
- Not letting go may be founded on a sense that there are tasks a person has yet to do on earth.
- Not letting go may be based on feelings of obligation to a person on earth.

The Departures

I kept company with Harry and Rosemary many years before when Rosemary and I worked together as nurses in an intensive-care unit. We bonded, sharing critical life-and-death events. Although the couple had moved to Arizona so they could live in a dry climate, we kept regular contact through letter writing. Rosemary was a very good nurse, full of energy, caring and smart about how to get things done. Her husband, Harry, only fifty-three years old, was crippled by emphysema, a disease that makes it hard for a person to breathe. He could no longer work. Harry spent his days waiting, tethered to an oxygen tank on wheels. Their story illustrates two themes. First, people may not want to let go and die because they feel strongly connected with loved ones. Second, letting go may come for these people only when those they love give them permission to die.

The phone call I received from Rosemary surprised me. Rosemary's voice trembled and was choked with tears. She cried out that Harry had died. She said, "I let him die." Then Rosemary wept as she recounted to me the events that led up to Harry's death.

Several times, in the past year, Harry had to be hospitalized on a breathing machine called a ventilator. His heart, too, had been damaged because it was overworked trying to make up for the weakened condition of his lungs.

One day Rosemary was called to Harry's bedside when things looked really dicey. He had the breathing machine tube down his throat so he couldn't speak. Harry's heart rate and rhythm had been vacillating. The nurses were puzzled as they watched Harry's erratic heart activity on the cardiac monitor. There seemed to be a pattern to its instability. When Harry's heart went to into an irregular pattern and Rose would comfort him by stroking his forehead, his heart beat would return to normal.

After weeks of mechanical ventilation of his lungs, Harry was weaned gradually from the machine and was finally able to talk. He told Rosemary that, while he was on the breathing machine, his spirit had taken trips. Harry went on to tell her about the trips. He said he left his body and hovered over the bed. Sometimes he'd go down a tunnel where there was light and warmth and love. Once he left and saw his father who had died five years before. He talked to his father about staying on the other side. But, when he saw Rosemary at the side of his bed where his body lay, he felt a tremendous pull toward her and came back into his body. He came back to Rosemary.

Harry's body became more and more debilitated by emphysema. Several years later he felt he could no longer go on. He was dependent on the oxygen machine he carted behind him most all the time. He could walk only twenty feet before needing to sit and rest. And, most important, he could no longer enjoy life with Rosemary.

That fall, although he ate sparsely during those days, Harry insisted on taking Rosemary out for dinner. As they enjoyed each other's company, Harry made his plea. "I want to go, Rosemary. I cannot be who I want to be any more. Please, the next time I am leaving—when the nurses say my heart rhythm is haywire—stay away from the bed. Do not touch me and pull me back. Let me go."

Harry was again hospitalized—just before Christmas— three months after talking with Rosemary about wanting to journey beyond life. Rosemary did as he asked, for she loved Harry. She cried hysterically as they took Harry's body away. She had let him go.

Rosemary said she phoned me tell me about the funeral arrangements. I believe Rosemary called also seeking validation that she had done the proper thing in letting Harry go. She needed a friend—a fellow nurse—to say it was all right, even a good deed, to let Harry depart.

He Shook His Head, "No."

Anita and I worked as nurses together on a medical unit. It was here Anita came upon her first encounter with a patient who wanted to stay over on the other side. Anita went in to do a dressing change for Stanley. This patient had been injured in a car rollover the month before. She always found it a delight to help this eighty-year-old man. Stanley was charming. His sense of humor and graciousness glowed through the multiple, harsh injuries he sustained. He never missed thanking people who cared for him. He acknowledged their smile, and the extra time they spent with him. Anita described how she cared for Stanley one particular day.

This event occurred sometime in Anita's third week as Stanley's nurse. The scene that greeted her that afternoon was unexpected. When she knocked on the door before entering Stanley's room, a weak groan was all she heard in reply. She ran to his bedside and shouted his name several times. He wasn't breathing. She could not find a pulse. She immediately pressed the alarm button to alert other staff to the problem.

Anita started CPR. As she opened his airway, Stanley clearly shook his head as if to make her move her hands away. But Anita did not stop. She breathed for Stanley. She pressed on his chest. CPR continued and a resuscitation routine with drugs was begun when others arrived on the scene.

During this emergency, Stanley's heart was beating erratically. Medication to calm his heart rhythm was started. He was connected to a machine which pushed air in and out of his lungs—breathed for him—so he could conserve what remained of his precious energy.

For more than six hours Stanley was attached to the breathing machine. The tube in his throat made it impossible for him to speak. But Stanley's heart rhythm eventually returned to normal and doctors were able to take the breathing tube out.

Afterward, Anita told Stanley how happy she was to see him awake and alert. She was shocked when he told her how he felt about it. He told Anita she had "no right, no right at all," to hold him back. "You pulled me back into my body with all that pressing down on my chest." Stanley complained. "I watched you. I wanted to yell at you to stop, that I was already on my way. I was feeling so peaceful. For the first time in a long time, I had no pain," he went on to say. Stanley, true to his nature, told Anita he was not angry at her. He was disappointed to be back. The next week, Stanley died quietly in his sleep, without any further CPR or drugs. He had made known his request: Do not resuscitate.

Anita cannot forget this story because she feels responsible for hurting this wonderful old man. She knows she has the tools and the skills, the gift to restore life. But now she wonders how appropriate it is to use them simply because they are available. Stanley's death heightened Anita's sensitivity to patients' wishes when death is near. She periodically reviews with patients their wishes regarding CPR. She knows that patients' wishes can change.

Anita now makes every effort to allow family and close friends to be in the room when death approaches. She knows that any patient, when critically ill, like Stanley, can then look down when leaving the body and, as a spirit, observe and hear those left behind. This experience taught Anita to accept death as part of life and of nursing care.

They Robbed Me of Death

Eunice, an RN, was staffing the emergency room when Mollie was brought in. The 74-year-old woman had collapsed at home, but had returned from death, thanks to the quick response of her family and the competence of the ambulance staff that had rushed to her aid. Mollie was medically unstable, but coherent. Eunice remembers Mollie's last few days, when she longed to die, as going like this.

"Please," Mollie pleaded with Eunice. "Don't let them do all this to me. I did not want them to help me. Death was robbed from me. I was fine. I was at peace. I did not want to live. I was not in pain until I woke up. They broke my rib, you know. It hurts now. I saw the light. It was warm. I want to go back."

Mollie and Eunice talked about letting go of life. Mollie was emphatic that she was ready to go. She had lived as long as she wanted.

Eunice relayed Mollie's wishes to the physician in charge. The doctor talked to Mollie about what she wanted done if she should collapse again. Molly formally became a "no code," which meant that if she should stop breathing or her heart stop, no resuscitation measures would be undertaken.

A few days later Mollie died. Eunice saw her comfortably and peacefully take her final breath. Eunice was glad Mollie could be where she wanted, with the warmth, peace, comfort, and light. Eunice shared with the family what Mollie had told her she experienced before when she journed beyond life: the light . . . warmth . . . peace.

Eunice says there is beauty in the fact that people can choose to have no medical interventions thrust upon them as they make their final entrance.

Just Someone with Me

As a nursing instructor at a large university, I was teaching student nurses on a busy hospital unit with patients who have a lot of problems. These patients were not hospitalized because of heart attacks or impending surgeries. Heart attacks and most surgeries call for a set pattern of nursing actions. No, these patients had multiple interactive and complex conditions. And the question often became one of prioritizing . . . "What should we treat first? What do we need to do first? "In this story, the patient seeks health care support for himself and his wife before finally letting go.

It was hectic the day when the unit clerk announced that George was in the Emergency Room and would be brought up to the floor soon. We all knew George. He had been a patient many times on this unit. Terminally ill with lung cancer, he had gone home to die. There was nothing more the doctors felt they could do. If George was back, it was because the end was near for him.

My nursing students were at that stage of development where they began to understand that a nurse's responsibility can extend beyond the patient. They were starting to see that the patient's family also had needs that nurses could meet. I knew that Betty, George's wife, had brought him in to the hospital. Since I wanted the students to see what it was like for a family member at this critical time, I volunteered my student group to take care of George.

Betty was at George's side as he was wheeled onto the Medical 4 unit. Tears filled her eyes. She brought George in because she sensed he was dying. He was not comfortable at home. She was at a loss as to what to do for him at home. She was afraid to be alone with him at death.

Physicians quickly gave a raft of orders. The student nurses were to suction his lungs, start oxygen, give medication for fever, draw blood for lab tests, and prepare the patient for X-ray.

I was talking with Betty as the students came breathlessly to the doorway. They stood still, watched, and listened. I held Betty's hand and she sobbed on my shoulder. She had done all she could, she cried. She was tired. He was tired. Betty said George was not acting like himself. He had been talking all night. He kept repeating his father's name. His father had died years before. I recognized George's talking to someone on the other side as a sign of impending death.

I asked the students to stand back for a minute. I sat on the bed close to George and said I wanted to help him in any way I could. George was short of breath, using all his energy and muscles just to move air in and out of his lungs. His skin was that combination of bluish-reddish-tan that is a sure sign his body was in deep trouble. The students ran to get the needed equipment. This was their first real emergency situation. It took only minutes to assemble everything needed to "take care of" George. I held George's hand and looked into in the eyes. He said, "Please hold me." And so I did. George's respiration became steady and regular. Even though a huge amount of technology was available to intervene with incredible swiftness, it was the presence of another human being that was most important to the patient. The students learned a valuable lesson. They found that they could be instruments of comfort. And they discovered that bringing comfort can have physiological side effects, such as lessening labored breathing in a patient.

The blood work and the X-ray merely confirmed what Betty and George both knew. He was dying. It appeared that Betty and George had come back to the hospital because they needed health-care professionals to be with them for support when George let go. As the day moved along, Betty was able to feel renewed and she regained some strength. Betty's conversation with George became more lively. She talked about the good times they shared. George could see that Betty was feeling more herself after having become exhausted at home by the demands of his illness. George knew the hospital staff well through his many stays with them. He whispered to the head nurse, "Make sure Betty gets home okay, please." Later that day, George lay back on his pillow and sighed. Betty embraced her husband as he died. Then it was her turn to be held. Staff comforted her.

Searching for Death

Bruce was a psychiatric nurse. In his job he often validated for patients what was real versus what was not real. His patients were medically stable so they did not die in the hospital. His first experience with death occurred when his mother, Selma, died. Bruce described Selma as a victim of Alzheimer's. Even though he was a nurse and knew better, he could not rid himself of the hope that her non-responsive state would pass and he could once again talk to this wonderful woman who had raised him. But Selma had been unable for years to form a complete sentence.

One evening as Bruce sat reading by his mother's bedside, he noticed Selma open her eyes wide. Her eyes darted around the room. She seemed panicked. "I can't find the light. I'm scared," she said clearly. It felt natural for Bruce to bring her close to him and reassure her that she would find the light.

Selma talked on and off for hours that night about seeing the light in the distance and wanting to get closer to it. Bruce kept corroborating she would find the light. Selma died the next day.

Bruce was saddened that his mother worried so much about finding the light she was seeking. Yet, he found it a relief to think that his mother, in the end, even though her mind's circuits were jumbled by Alzheimer's, knew that a comforting light was there for her. He says he is sure that she found it.

This personal episode confirmed Bruce's professional philosophy that a nurse should listen to patients at the edge of death and talk to them about what they see. Nurses validating the light that dying often see may be comforting. When patients at the edge of death talk about searching for the light, Bruce hopes they will be reassured and told they will find it.

Let Him Go

Judy was Vic's primary nurse. She had nursed him since he was transferred from the intensive care unit to the medical neurology unit where she worked. Vic had not only a brain tumor but also many other complex skin care problems. He needed 24-hour care with specialized treatments and a unique bed that could turn him completely over every hour. And so it was decided that Vic would remain in the hospital for the duration of his life.

Being Vic's primary nurse meant Judy planned his care, carried it out when she was working, and evaluated his response to medical and nursing interventions. It took some collaboration. Judy learned what Vic liked best and at what times he wanted things done. She tried to do what she could to make things happen when he wanted. She was his advocate. She watched out for him.

As Judy came on one night, Vic's wife met her at the nursing station. She asked how soon Judy would go in to see her husband. Judy said she would go right in. She could tell by his shallow breathing that Vic was experiencing respiratory distress. There were long periods between each breath. He gasped and jerked as he caught a breath. A gurgling noise could be heard when air went in and out.

Although the decision to not perform heroic measures had been made and documented, Judy suggested she stimulate him to breathe more fully by suctioning him. "No," said the wife. "I know he doesn't want that. He told me to get you when you came on. He has been waiting for you to come on so you could be here when he dies." Judy sat down at the foot of the bed and held the wife's hand.

Judy sat for a while, and then went out and took care of other patients. She returned many times during the shift. Each time she came back into the room, she took the wife's hand and gently stroked it, saying to her that Vic looked at peace. Judy was present when Vic died. She sensed a heaviness lifting upward as Vic's spirit left his body. When she looked at Vic's wife, she could see relief also on her face.

As death approached Judy did what the patient wanted. Judy waited for his passing on with the loved one the patient left behind.

Life-Death-Life

Gary is a paramedic who believes that death is as much a beginning as an ending. When responding to a call to rescue an elderly woman with chest pain, he met Tena. Gary tells this story about the rescue call and the patient's wish just to have someone with her when she died.

"I'm dying, you know. My brother is here with me. I'm dying," Tena whispered matter-of-factly. Gary had arrived at Tena's apartment only moments before. Tena was lying on the couch. Gary was unable to hear a blood pressure. He scrambled to get electrocardiogram leads on her chest. "I just called so

someone would be here with me. God has come to take me."
Tena interjected. "I am 96 years old and ready to die."

But Gary was not fully listening or responding to Tena's
words. His attention was distracted to the intravenous line (IV)
he was placing. He replaced the oxygen mask that Tena had
pushed away from her mouth and nose.

Tena pushed away the mask. "Thank you, but I'm dying,"
Tena said again. Gary begged Tena to stop fidgeting with the
equipment and to cooperate with wearing the mask. But finally,
after placing the mask several times, he called in to his supervisor, "Patient refuses oxygen. She keeps taking the mask off. I
think I'll need to restrain her."

With a roll of gauze, Gary bound Tena's hands down onto
the stretcher. It bothered Gary to tie down Tena's hands so she
could not take off the oxygen mask. She was so frail, so fragile.
He worried that the gauze would tear into her skin as she tried
to move her hands. Elderly skin, he thought, is like rice paper—
it tears so easily.

Gary then knew that Tena was telling him that death was
coming for her. He, other times, had heard the dying, like Tena,
talk about relatives coming to meet them to take them to heaven.
They let go of this life to join the person who had passed away
before. Even though he must follow protocol and carry out specific emergency routines, Gary communicates respect for each
person he rescues. He sensed Tena's need to have someone with
her and that's why he believed she dialed 911 even though she
knew she was dying. So he said to Tena after he restrained her
hands, "You seem to know where you are going. Wherever you
are going you will be well taken care of." Tena died shortly after
transportation to the hospital.

Some of Gary's patients live and others die. "Sometimes I
save lives," says Gary, "and other times I am here to preserve

the dignity of people who just want someone with them when they die."

If It Comes, It Comes

Lillian cared for her brother Walter's children when his wife died forty years ago and left him a widower with three young girls. She moved into Walter's house when the children were little and stayed on long after they grew up and moved away. She knew Walter's ways. Sometimes family members are asked by physicians to give them direction whether to pursue medical treatment vigorously or to let a person pass on. Lillian shares this vignette of how she relayed her brother's wishes so that he could die and join his deceased wife.

Lillian threw her hands up in despair and cried out in response to Doctor Shore's questions about her older brother Walter, "He is suffering so much. There is no rhyme or reason. He has already died once. Why all this?" Walter had had open heart surgery three months previously. He was lucky to make it through the operation. His heart had stopped three times before they wheeled him into the surgical suite.

After one of those times when Walter received CPR, he told Lillian a story about his journey beyond life. He said he went through a tunnel and found himself wrapped totally in a bright light. He said he saw heaven. He described the place as the most beautiful he had ever seen. Walter cried when he told Lillian that Elsa, his wife, met him and said, "It's not your time. Go back." He didn't want to leave her. He did not want to come back. Walter told Lillian not to worry if he dies, "If it comes, it comes," he said. "I'll be happy to be with Elsa."

Two and a half months after the heart surgery, when a clot traveled to Walter's brain, he collapsed. He never regained consciousness. Doctor Shore looked to Lillian for some direction. She asked if Lillian knew what Bob would want if he could speak.

Lillian knew her brother to be a proud and fiercely independent man. When the doctors explained the meaning of the brain studies, that Walter would never recover his mental faculties, Lillian said, "Walter would want death to come now."

Because of Lillian's input, Doctor Shore decided to not treat Walter vigorously. Instead, a comfort care plan was started . . . acetaminophen for fever, oral hygiene every two hours, frequent repositioning, skin cares. For two more weeks Lillian was at her brother's bedside. She lamented that Walter went through so much only to be dying.

But when Walter passed on in his sleep, Lillian said she realized that illness had taught her brother what the next life is like. He came to understand that death is not to be feared and would come sometime unanounced.

Research has shown that cardiopulmonary resuscitation (CPR) has limited use for the elderly with multisystem problems. Few survive. Those who survive most often do not regain their prior level of functioning. Unless you witness a cardiac arrest and start CPR immediately and have other life support measures available, physician experts advise against putting an elderly, frail person through it. More often than not, no reasonable benefit can be expected.

Most people would want CPR if they liked their current level of health and functioning and CPR was *guaranteed* to be *free* and *painless* and *successful* in returning them to the way they normally function in life. But CPR for the elderly carries some big burdens: high cost, pain, and no guarantees. On the average, only two percent of nursing home residents, with a mean age of 82, survive CPR (Duthie and Tresch, 1993).

I am practically dead,
but you keep me alive,
treating my heart with pills.

I am practically dead,
but you keep me alive.
My breathing attests to your skills.

I am practically dead,
but you keep me alive
against my own free will.

I want to die.
I've seen the Light.
Go away! Hands off! Be still!

CHAPTER SIX

Comfort Care

It takes one human being who really cares
to make a difference between life and death.
—ELISABETH KUBLER-ROSS

Accumulating information about near-death experiences is one thing, but incorporating this information into a professional nursing practice is quite another. I have found that applying the lessons I have learned is like a journey across rapids. The gap between knowledge and action is fraught with uncertainties and barriers. One must take chances to learn how best to traverse the waters.

My sharing experiences people have had with death has improved and expanded my capacity to provide nursing care for patients and their families. Through story sharing, I can more knowledgably and convincingly reassure patients who are dying and comfort families and friends left behind to deal with death.

I have purposely let it be known that I will talk to people about death. Although there still exists a taboo against discussing death, talking about deathbed and near-death experiences has proven to be an entry that allows people to explore their own feelings. When someone dies unexpectedly and suddenly, we know the question families ask most often is, "Did my family member suffer in the end?" Near-death experiences provide an answer. Sharing near-death events encourages talk about the process of dying.

People let nurses know what is on their minds because our education in psychology and social sciences prepares nurses to make situations safe for people to tell us who they really are. We, as nurses, accept people unconditionally, nonjudgmentally, with all their faults. We often are given opportunity not afforded others to see beneath fear, shyness, audacity, and, even, vitriolic outbursts, and to learn what is on the minds of our patients. Nursing is not only a science but is also the art of interacting with another human being.

When I am called to the side of a dying person or, for that matter, to the side of someone who has experienced the death of another, I hasten to explain that what I have to say is intended to be comforting. I am there to share stories that people have told me about going over to the other side. I am also there so the person has someone with whom to discuss thoughts and feelings. Let me give you some examples from my practice.

> *God uses our efforts to show*
> *His love to people around us.*
> —BILL WINEKE

The air itself seems uncomfortably heavy when a child has died. A cloak of sadness enshrouds everyone and everything around. A child's death is so gut-wrenching, it seem as if a huge part of the parents' very own bodies has been torn from them. There is a sense of despair as deep as any with which I have ever come into contact. Every person and every conversation is weighted down when a child dies.

A Sudden Infant Death Syndrome (SIDS) baby arrived at the emergency department one afternoon. When the infant arrived, the parents were still on their way to the hospital from work. Their babysitter had told them that their little girl had been brought to the hospital, but no one had told them what had happened. I went to meet them.

"Not my Jennie! Not my Jennie!" the father cried.

The mother sat, put her head down and wept. When she looked up, her stare was vacant, as if her presence was in another world. The father put his arm around her and the mother buried her head on his chest.

The doctor on duty briefly explained what few details were known and gave an indication of the tests that would be done. The coroner comforted the mother and father. He told them he would stop by their home the next day with information gained from the autopsy. After the physician left, the couple sat and talked with the minister and me. The minister said things would be all right and that God would help them through this.

The father's eyes showed that terror had suddenly been added to disbelief. The father said "My Jennie was never baptized. We meant to get it done. But we didn't. What will happen to her now?" The minister calmly explained that in this life, we often do not do everything we set out to do. Many times we have good intentions, but we do not always carry them through. Life is difficult. He explained there are many daily pressures that lay stress on us. "God understands we do not get everything done we want to. He also understands when we are trying," the minister said.

I told the couple about patients of mine who were not religious, but, because of a near-death event, learned there was a life for them after death. These people did not have formal religious training or induction ceremonies, but found that they were welcomed into a life beyond.

A new surge of questions spewed forth. "How did she die?," the mother whispered. We had no answers. We could only repeat that the coroner was going to investigate and would tell them what he knew the next day. "My poor Jennie," the father cried. "Did she choke? Did she cry?" It was obvious that he was worried about how Jennie felt as she died. I told him that people who passed over to death and returned said that there was no pain at all during the experience and that we could be reasonably sure there was none for baby Jennie.

"She was so little," cried her father, "and I have lost both my parents this year too." I told them that many people report being met in the next life by people who have gone before—many times, relatives. The father's face brightened; he managed a small smile and said to his wife, "Maybe, Dad and Mom met Jennie and are with her. Oh, I hope so."

Glimpses of death that people shared with me were now helping a family deal with a world unknown to them. Perhaps this is one of the reasons near-death events occur—that others whose lives are touched by death may be comforted.

> *Man can find meaning in suffering*
> *And can transcend what fate bestows.*
> —Viktor Frankl

The young man looked up and offered me a place to sit. His parents had asked me to speak with him after his motorcycle accident because, after he was resuscitated, he talked about seeing God. They had heard about near-death experiences and were wondering if their son Scott's story was true.

I introduced the topic to Scott by explaining that I often talked to people who had been in accidents and that sometimes they told me of unusual experiences after the crash. I asked what it was like for him. Scott began by giving a detailed account of the circumstances: the day of the week; the weather; the fact that the sun had been in his eyes; the emergency room; and how frightened his parents looked as the doctors and nurses were working on him. I knew that he had been unconscious when he arrived, so I asked him how he could see his parents' faces. He replied, after some hesitation, "I guess I was above looking down at me in the bed and my parents by the door. Do you believe me?"

"Yes, I believe you," I said, "and you are not alone in having this happen to you in an emergency room. Lots of people report being out of their bodies looking down over the emergency room staff as they worked. This happens. Did anything else unusual happen?"

Scott told me how all of a sudden he found himself going through a tunnel and at the end he met a person who looked to him like God. He said "God told me it wasn't my time." Then Scott said he popped suddenly back into his body and could feel pain in his leg that was severed in the accident.

"Do you think I am going crazy because of the medicine they are giving me?," Scott asked me. I told him I did not believe the medicine was making him hallucinate, but rather that he had a near-death experience. He said he was afraid to talk about it with his parents. The picture of them huddled together in the emergency room was etched in his mind. He did not want to see them worried about his mental condition as well.

He asked me to tell him more about near-death experiences. The more I told him about the characteristics, the more he relaxed. He lay back down on the hospital bed and stared into space a long time. He asked if I could be there when he talked with his parents about his near-death experience and if I would reassure them, as I did him, that people who have near-death experiences are not more likely to die in the near future than those who do not.

The next week, Scott and his parents and I met. I explained that their son had experienced a number of the characteristics of a near-death experience. Scott concurred and said that he had more to add. He had been thinking a lot about why he might have been lucky enough to survive the accident and get a look at death. He said he decided to go back to school. He had seen the genuine satisfaction that nurses, nursing assistants, and technicians got from their work every day. He wanted to go to technical school so he could work in the health-care field and help other people the way he had been helped since the accident.

Scott had been hopping from one job to another since high school. His parents were ecstatic that he was interested in getting more education. This family started to make plans for the young man to enroll in a school near their home. By talking about death, Scott had come to face what he wanted to do with the rest of his life. This significant event taught a young man that he wanted his life's work to be meaningful.

Eternity is not something
that begins after you die.
You are in it now.

"Your wife and I will stay with you," I said to Mr. Bergen, the 81-year-old man who, although breathing jerkily, lay quietly with his eyes closed. The staff physician and two residents had just left the room after disconnecting his ventilator and removing the endotracheal tube and intravenous lines.

I asked a staff member to bring a chair for his wife. Her fingers were digging tightly into my hand. It isn't easy or comfortable to watch preparations for death even when you are the one requesting it, as she had. I certainly didn't want to leave her alone.

Mr. Bergen had arrived by ambulance three days before. He had been intubated (a tube put into his airway) in the ambulance and placed on a ventilator when he arrived in the intensive care unit.

It had all started when Mr. Bergen collapsed at home. Following Mrs. Bergen's 911 call, rescuers swiftly arranged for transportation to the hospital. Mrs. Bergen went back into the house to get her husband's Health Care Power of Attorney. Then she drove to the hospital. By the time Mrs. Bergen arrived, nurses and doctors were busily giving Mr. Bergen stabilizing drugs. She didn't want to interrupt their frantic work, so she paced back and forth outside the room.

A doctor came out to give Mrs. Bergen a status report: "Stable. On a breathing machine. Unresponsive; in a coma. Probably a massive stroke." She took the papers out of her purse. The directives read: "No mechanical support. No CPR." The doctor said life support had started when she called 911 and the doctors couldn't stop now. Mrs. Bergen broke down and wept.

A nurse observing the events called to tell me of the dilemma. When I met Mrs. Bergen she was still clutching the papers. She held them out for me to read. She was still crying while she pleaded, "William didn't want this; he really didn't want this!"

Mrs. Bergen and I talked through the events of the day and I explained why the paramedics had to put a tube down and place IVs. The explanation did little to reduce Mrs. Bergen's despair. "I let him down," she sobbed. "We had promised each other none of this."

I contacted Mr. Bergen's personal physician. When he called back, he said there was nothing he could do to have the tubes removed. I met with the staff physician and residents and pleaded Mrs. Bergen's case. The staff man said he'd do studies and consider removing the life support if the findings showed irreversible brain damage.

In the meantime two days passed. Mrs. Bergen contacted the children who both supported their father's previously written choice. On the third day, the medical staff concurred and removed all the tubes.

It was then that death could be the event as planned for by the couple. I told Mrs. Bergen that people who are in comas may hear and understand even though they do not open their eyes and respond. I also said that some people, who have been near-death report also being able to see those at their bedside. Sometimes, critically ill people leave their bodies and their spirit hovers above and looks down.

Mrs. Bergen stroked her husband's head. She asked me to comb his hair so it looked the way he liked it. She held his hand while I went out to get us sandwiches. Later she rested her head on his chest. She told him she loved him. She explained that she had talked to the children and they said good-bye. After ten hours his breathing became more shallow and he finally stopped breathing. She was tired but pleased that the end was calm and unencumbered, as he wanted.

I am convinced that touching and talking to someone at death may provide equal shares of comfort for the dying and for those left behind.

> *The most healing things that we can do*
> *with someone who is in pain,*
> *rather than trying to get rid of that pain,*
> *is to sit there and be willing to share it.*
> —M. SCOTT PECK

Christine, a young mother, had awakened in the recovery room after emergency surgery. The driver of a truck ran a stop sign and hit Christine's car broadside. The mother's arms and collarbone were broken. Her ankle was fractured. She was badly bruised. Her eyes were swollen almost completely shut. It was only after awakening from surgery that she found out her eight-year-old daughter had died at the scene.

Christine's nurse called me, although I worked at a different facility, and told me that her patient wanted to know more about death. When I knocked on the door to Christine's room, her husband Mark answered. I told him Christine's nurse had called me because she knew I studied people who had died, journeyed beyond life, and come back. The nurse said Christine wanted to hear from me what people said death was like. I said I could share, if they would like, what other people who had been in accidents or had serious illness told me happened to them when they passed over to the other side.

I checked to make sure they wanted me there. "Yes," he whispered, "She very much wants to see you, and I do, too." The shades were pulled in the room and I found it hard to see as I made my way over to the bed. The room was quiet. Mark followed.

Christine looked very, very tired. She did not move except to say, "Please talk to me. I want to know." I began by telling the elements of near-death experiences and how widespread the occurrence of NDEs is. I recounted what kinds of things other accident victims remembered. Christine listened intently and looked up at me though her eyes were barely open. Keeping her eyes open just a bit seemed like a big effort. I could tell that this information meant a lot to her. She wanted desperately to know about death. Mark rubbed her hand.

Then I told Christine and Mark stories children had related after they had been declared clinically dead but later had come back to life. When I told Christine about how people are met by relatives and friends, she looked over at her husband. He said, "Maybe Grandma Mary." She said, "And Grandma Mae." He said that these women were two of their favorite people. They talked about the grandmothers. That their daughter would have been met by one or both seemed a source of comfort to them.

Christine had been thrown out of the car away from her daughter at the time of the accident. She was taken in a separate ambulance to the hospital. Mark identified the child in the morgue. He said he was horrified at her injuries. That people said they suffered no pain when they nearly died was meaningful to him. He had been waking up with terrifying nightmares, writhing with feelings of the pain he had thought his daughter must have suffered in the end. Now he could challenge those thoughts.

Talking with this couple about near-death events allayed some of their greatest fears: who was taking care of their daughter and did their daughter suffer in the end? Even though their child wasn't with them, Christine and Mark's pain was eased because they now felt that she was in a comfortable and good place.

> *To be completely honest with oneself*
> *is the very best effort*
> *a human being can make.*
> —SIGMUND FREUD

I met Robert in the visitors' lounge outside the room where his wife was recovering from an automobile accident. Robert had been driving; his wife and son were passengers. His son Tyrone had been killed.

Robert stood up to shake my hand and then put his hands on his forehead and held it as he talked to me. "How could this be? Have I done something wrong? Why bad luck now when my life seemed to be going so well?" Robert's wife had told me she was concerned about him, and it appeared that she was justified. He blamed himself for the car accident. He blamed himself for the death of their son.

I pointed out that accidents and death were unpredictable and, in many cases, unavoidable. Bad things happen to good people. Bad things can happen to anyone. I tried to reassure Robert that he hadn't done anything wrong. His son had been seatbelted. Ice had simply formed very quickly that night and the sudden slickness had caught many drivers by surprise.

He pressed me as to what I thought it was like for his son, Tyrone. Robert wanted to know how much of the accident Tyrone would have seen. Would he have seen his mother being crushed in the front seat? I began by telling Robert what people in accidents often told me, that they leave their bodies and look at the scene from above. I reassured Robert that accident victims say there is no feeling of pain when they are out of their bodies, even though they have injuries. We talked further— about the tunnel, the light, the relatives and friends who gather and greet the dead.

"Do you think that when I die Tyrone will be waiting there for me? Do you think I will see his sweet face again when I die? I would like to think that he will be waiting for me," Robert said. I told Robert that's a good thought to hold on to. I told him I believe from what I've heard that we are reunited at death with those we love. I said we can continue to love those who have died and keep a spiritual connection with people on the other side. Tyrone did not have to be forgotten.

We talked for hours about the little boy that Robert loved so much. Robert described Tyrone's favorite toys, his love of the zoo and of swinging the highest he could be pushed on a swing. He described the blanket Tyrone cuddled every time he slept. Robert shared his favorite memories, the lovable quirks his son had, the dreams that would never now come true. An empty bedroom haunted Robert's mind. Robert's life was broken.

Robert asked me to go with him and share with his parents and sisters what we had talked about, where I thought Tyrone was. As we got up to go do so, he held on to me for a long time. Then Robert said, with a deep sigh, "I wish I had never met you. Then, after a pause, he explained, "It's not like I don't like you, because I do. You've helped me today. Now I can picture Tyrone waiting for me in heaven instead of just seeing that empty room of his. I can think of a future when I will see him again. But I wish I never met you because that would mean this all never happened . . . that the accident didn't happen . . . that my son is not dead. I wish I never had to meet you, but I'm glad you came. Thank you."

Comfort care, that's what I give. I share what a near-death experience is like. I tell the stories I've been told and let people draw from them what is important and meaningful for them. I always find there is a purpose to it all. For the dying, it's comforting. For the living, it's comforting.

CHAPTER SEVEN

Facts and Beliefs

*Facts do not cease to exist
because they are ignored.*
—ALDOUS HUXLEY

I have tested hundreds of health care workers—nurses, pharmacists, physicians, respiratory therapists, morticians, and emergency medical personnel. They have been up-front about what they know and believe about near-death experiences. Here are the questions I asked them. You may want to test yourself and see how you compare.

Directions: Circle the T (true) or F (false) answer which most nearly agrees with your view.

T F 1. Thirty-five percent of adult Americans who have come close to death report having a near-death experience.

T F 2. Most people who report near-death experiences say they no longer fear death.

T F   3. Suicide attempters who have near-death experiences are less likely to attempt suicide again.

T F   4. Most people who have near-death experiences are less concerned with material possessions afterwards.

T F   5. Ancient civilizations induced a type of near-death experience to teach people that there is a spirit which lives on after death.

T F   6. Near-death experiences are more likely to occur when the survivor's length of unconsciousness is greater than thirty minutes.

T F   7. Near-death experiences are more likely where the methods used to resuscitate the survivor are extensive.

T F   8. After a near-death experience, people are likely to report a sense of loss at having to give up the incredible beauty and peace they met in the "other world."

T F   9. Survivors report having a decreased need for formal religion after having a near-death experience.

T F 10. Survivors of near-death experiences may feel emotionally isolated from family and friends who may not understand the event.

T F 11. Patients who have undergone cardiopulmonary resuscitation have later reported seeing and hearing the callous or offensive behavior of emergency staff.

T F 12. Out-of-body experiences have been documented in every time and culture.

T F 13. Seventy percent of Americans believe in an afterlife.

T F 14. Three out of ten Americans report that they have had an out-of-body experience.

T F 15. One in four Americans believe in reincarnation.

T F 16. Children, as well as adults, report near-death experiences.

All answers to the questions are TRUE.

Questions people most often get wrong are:

#6.   It is true that a near-death experience is more likely to occur if one is unconscious longer.

#9.   It is true that survivors claim a reduced need for formal religion after a near-death experience. But near-death experiencers say they are more spiritual.

#10. It is true that survivors of near-death experiences often feel emotionally isolated from family and friends.

#14. It is true that three out of ten Americans admit to having had an out-of-body experience.

You can match your beliefs to what is known to be true. Discuss with your family and friends what they have experienced and what they believe.

Knowing the truth may set you free to help those who have a brush with death or are dying. Hospitals are not always hospitable, but people—like you—can make the hospital stage a friendlier entrance to the other world.

Near-death Experiences in Patients Undergoing Cardiopulmonary Resuscitation

I have studied the frequency of near-death experiences in patients who have had CPR done to them. The purposes of this study were to reveal the frequency of near-death experiences in a nonprobability convenience sample of patients undergoing CPR; to describe the type of NDE experienced; and to describe patients' views of a helpful nursing response to reports of NDEs.

For this research, the sample was patients who were admitted to an acute-care hospital in the Midwest. All patients and their physicians agreed the patients could be interviewed about the feelings and perceptions they had while the CPR experience was going on.

Subjects answered questions on Greyson's NDE measurement tool and were further interviewed about helpful nursing follow-up. Greyson's scale is a sixteen-item instrument that reviews elements of the near-death experience. The section of the questionnaire that deals with the cognitive aspects of the near-death experience asks the person if time distortion, thought acceleration, life review, or sudden understanding occurred. Questions about affective elements of the near-death experience review the person's feelings of peace, joy, cosmic unity, and the light. A section of questions about paranormal happenings asks if the experiencer had enhanced vision or hearing, extrasensory perception, precognition, or an out-of-body experience. Questions about the transcendental aspects cover the areas of being in an unearthly realm, encountering unearthly beings or spirits, and coming to a barrier. This tool has internal consistency of .88 on Cronbach's Alpha and .84 Pearson R for test-retest reliability.

Eleven people participated in the study. Five out of the eleven reported some elements of the near-death experience occurred to them while CPR was done. One person said that he met with God.

It seems reasonable that health care workers become familiar and ready to respond to significant life events which appear to happen to a great number of people. A report of this study appears in the *Journal of Near-Death Studies*, volume 9, issue 4, Summer 1991.

Physiological Explanations

Although millions of people see their near-death experiences as being primarily spiritual in nature, scientists continue to propose physiological and psychological explanations for such events. I believe these are not necessarily contradictory propositions.

A near-death experience, by definition, is a spiritual experience of undetermined origin occurring when a person is in clinical death or in a situation of grave physical or psychological danger. NDE occurs with clinical death, not brain death. This is an important point to remember. Modern medicine can revive a person from clinical death. For someone to come back to life after brain death is humanly impossible.

The near-death experience can be a physiologically or psychologically produced experience that is a spiritually profound event. The measure of whether something is spiritually profound is not what causes it, or what triggers it, but rather, whether it is spiritual in nature and leads to spiritual understanding. Those who tell of near-death events often describe their experiences as the most significant events of their lives.

There are several explanations for near-death experiences that are popular with scientists.

Drug Theory

The brain is a beautiful apothecary. As the brain nears death, endorphins—the body's own narcotic—are released. Endorphin release can lead to feelings of euphoria, involuntary recall of memories, a sense of dissociation from the body, and hallucinations.

Hallucinogenic experiences have been associated with events similar to near-death experiences. As early as the 1800s, it was reported marijuana allowed the soul to explore the spiritual world. Marijuana has been called "heavenly guide" and "poor man's heaven" because of its association with the feeling of being out of one's body and in another world.

Oxygen Theory

Whatever the illness or trauma that initiates the chain of events that culminates in clinical death, the last common denominator is anoxia, i.e., lack of oxygen to the brain. Such lack of essential oxygen could cause tunnel vision and visual hallucinations.

Brain Activity Theory

When the brain's visual cortex is flooded with dots of light, a person has the sensation of moving forward through a tunnel. Some researchers feel the near-death experience is caused by such random activity of the brain at death.

Ego Defense Theory

Some psychologists claim that a person when faced with a life-threatening situation, may re-define the situation into an illusion that makes the situation seem more bearable. In this case, when a person is dying, the person envisions never dying, i.e., immortality. It is believed this illusion of immortality may have visual and auditory hallucination components.

CHAPTER EIGHT

Common Themes

He was a wise man who invented God.
—PLATO

What people tell us they see in death has remarkably recurring themes. This final entrance has common features: feelings of joy and peace and wonder, out-of-body and tunnel experiences, altered time, beautiful scenes, seeing family and friends who have died before, reviewing of deeds with guides and the being of light, and a border where return is decreed.

Death has been a life event known incompletely in the past. The stories of people who have had experiences with dying have brought forth new knowledge. Each description has given us clues that make meaning out of mystery. New beliefs have emerged, not from ancient scrolls or religious dogma, but from the voices of people who have heard, seen, and felt death.

That spirits come among us to help ease our entrance into death is a conviction held by those who die and their caregivers, family, and friends. Near-death experiencers report that they have taken on spiritual form beyond their bodily existence. Each says this spiritual form does not feel the physical sensations of a body, such as pain or cold. Others say they have sensed the presence of spiritual beings visiting at the bedside of the critically ill and have felt the dying's state-of-being transform into a spiritual presence as it lifts up from the body and leaves the room.

That corners of rooms are focal points for discussions between the dying and those who have gone before is consistently reported. People who have journeyed out of their bodies also tell us that corners are often the vantage spots from which they can view what is happening to their physical being.

And many tell us that they truly cherish their death as a life event they want no one to interfere with. Every person wants to give as much meaning to life as possible. We know man finds meaning not only when performing a service, or creating a work, but also when he, simply, experiences. That each of us may want to make a decision about how we experience death and when we die is a theme that cannot be ignored, but needs to be brought forward into family and health-care discussions.

Each of us is designated a time for our first entrance into this world. May the themes generated by stories in this book help you see your final entrance as a comma and not a period in the story of life.

CHAPTER NINE

What You Can Do

Even if you are on the right track,
You'll get run over if you just sit there.
—WILL ROGERS

W e all have wishes in our hearts and I will share with you one of mine. This is my wish, my hope: that you will think about the stories you've read and search for the awesome possibilities these reports present for you—in growing spiritually yourself and in helping others know about death.

Open yourself up to feeling the spirit. Spirits are all around us. Take some time by yourself alone. Find a place of natural beauty and quiet. Be still and know you are not alone, ever. Clear your mind of the day at hand. Be open. Allow the energies of nature to penetrate and renew you. Let spirits enter your thoughts and heart. As your awareness of you as a spirit grows, knowledge of the meaning of your life will also.

Decide what you believe about life after death. Death is a life event. Near-death experiencers say the event teaches us about an existence beyond death. What you believe about life after death can influence how you live your life.

Be with people and their families as death draws near. Remember that when a person dies, their spirit may float right above people around them. The spirit may look down as it leaves. Say the words you want heard. Communication is possible during the death event. You may take this opportunity to share your feelings. Many who experience the death of someone else say they feel a rush of wonderment and strength as the person exits.

Plan Your Final Entrance.

We prepare in all sorts of ways for special events in our lives. There are books that guide us to put on the "perfect" wedding day, execute the "best" job interview, and get the "top" score on entrance examinations. We follow the principle, "Fail to plan; plan to fail." Yes, Americans anticipate and rehearse for life events.

Our preparation for death—a monumental life event—comes up short by comparison. Choosing a burial site and coffin or cremation and urn is not enough. Planning these is like choosing props but no script for the play.

What do you need to tell your loved ones about how you want to die? Do you want to be resuscitated if your heart stops? Do you want to be fed with a tube if you cannot eat? Will you accept being on a breathing machine if it means forever? There are no right or wrong answers to these questions. Your answers count. You have the right to let your choices be known.

To plan your final entrance, consider these questions:

- With whom do I feel comfortable enough to disclose what I want my death to be like?
- Whom can I entrust to carry out my wishes?
- How can I legally ensure that my directions are followed?
- Is my Health Care Power of Attorney or Living Will up to date? Does it state clearly and specifically what I want and what I do not want?
- Whom do I want beside me as I die?
- Do I want to die in a hospital, nursing home, my home, or somewhere else?
- What do I want to eat or drink when I am near-death?
- What music or readings do I want to hear when I am dying?
- Which people would I like to speak to or see before I die?
- Is there a favorite cologne or scent I'd like to smell as I die?
- Do I want to be dressed in a specific outfit when I die?
- Do I want my hair fixed in a certain way when I die?
- Are there rituals I want performed as I die or immediately thereafter?

  Choices to consider:
  - ☐ funeral service   ☐ public ☐ family only
  - ☐ memorial service   ☐ public ☐ family only
  - ☐ cremation
  - ☐ burial ☐ where_____
  - ☐ memorial gifts in lieu of flowers: to whom/what?

- Who should be notified when I die? Who has the names and addresses and phone numbers and will do this?
- Will my obituary say what I think is important to say?
- Will I have asked forgiveness from those I have hurt intentionally or even unintentionally?
- Will I have said to the people I love all I think is important for them to know, or should I write it down in case my end

comes unexpectedly or I am incapacitated to the extent that I cannot speak or write?

- Who will take care of my estate?
- Who knows my social security number?
- Who has access to my savings/checking accounts?
- Who has access to my safe deposit box?
- Who has my will?
- Who has copies of my insurance policies/loans/deeds?
- Who will pay the final bills?

These next stories tell how two women met death surrounded by what was important to them.

Lois's Last Days

I cared for a woman who was dying of old age. Her heart was worn out. Her lungs and her kidneys functioned minimally. But her mind was sharp. She loved hot fudge sundaes and, until the day of her death, she ate them. Sometimes, since she was weak and had difficulty swallowing, she would just swirl the chocolate around in her mouth to savor the flavor. Her eyes and lips smiled with pleasure. She instructed that her radio be tuned to a religious station that played songs which comforted her. She told family, clergy, nurses and her doctor she was ready to die. She designed the stage for her final entrance.

The Look of Emily

Emily had been in the hospital four months when I met her. The prognosis was not good. It did not look as if she would be able to go home because there was no one to care for her there. Yet friends stopped in to see her. They brought her lovely gowns and robes because she was a woman who always wanted to look nice.

Emily's hair had been cut by the hospital beautician. That cost her a lot, she mentioned. She had tawny blonde color covering half her hair. Gray roots grew out from her scalp. When Emily looked in the mirror, you could see disappointment. You could feel her sadness. She was dying outside and inside.

I offered to bring in some hair coloring to try to match her roots to the ends of her hair. She looked astonished at first. I explained that I did know somewhat how to do it. So we made a bargain that the dye job would be done the next morning. I hid the chemicals under towels as we made our way to the shower room. After we put the "Do Not Disturb" sign up, we laughed at all our secrecy. We laughed like two high school girls coloring hair without our mothers' permission.

This hair dye was more than a vanity wish. This patient wanted to look like herself at death. She wanted to be the woman she had become in life so her final entrance would reflect her true self.

Honoring the Spirit

You never know when
You are making a memory.
—FRANK PERUGI

Our response to death can be to recognize its coming and participate in each occurrence. It is important to honor the dead, especially those with whom we've had long and caring relationships. Ceremony honoring the dead brings closure. Healthcare workers who become close to the dying report there is a special healing in saying good-bye at the bedside when someone dies. Families find comfort and solace as they listen to caregivers reminisce about times with their loved one.

I was taught about bedside closure services by Reverend Richard "Chappie" Horst, a Lutheran pastor in Destin, Florida. Bedside closure services can be led at the time of death by a pastoral or nonpastoral person. I am accustomed that the staff member who was closest to the dying person take the lead. At such services people gather around the bed of the person who has died. They share stories, memories of their contacts with the deceased. There may be tears. There may be laughter. There is a chance to express feelings, to say good-bye. The following stories give you a picture of how health-care workers can pay tribute and say their final good-byes to patients and family members.

Eddie and Jean

When Eddie died, his wife Jean was holding his hand. Both husband and wife had been residents, for many years, in the same room of the nursing home. The nurse had prepared Jean for Eddie's death. A nursing assistant stood behind Jean, giving her shoulders a light massage as they waited for Eddie's death to come.

As death often does, it came quietly and swiftly for Eddie. While a staff member stayed with Jean and with Eddie's body, other staff went about the tasks of notifying the physician, family, and funeral director, and cleansing the body.

Then the bedside service was held. Staff, including housekeepers, nursing, social services, dietary, activity, education, and administration personnel gathered around Eddie. We encirlced Jean. As she sat next to the body of her husband, there was an outpouring of messages.

The administrator told how he often observed the love the couple shared. A nurse spoke of how we knew that when Eddie or Jean was worried, the worry was always about the other one. People spoke about some of the things the couple did together.

Then we, all of different faiths, prayed together. We asked that comfort be given to Eddie as he passed on into another life. We asked that Jean be surrounded by those who shared her loss and would care for her. We gave thanks for the life this couple shared.

There were tears and smiles. After the service people went back to their work knowing they had a chance to say good-bye. Someone stayed with Jean to help her with the work of grieving.

Chapel Service

Melody was so loved. And this was because she was a loving person. Her radiance was like a flower that opened brightly each day and shed a petal wherever she went. She was nice to every-one. Everyone was warmed by the smile she gave when she wheeled through the halls of the nursing home.

When she died, a hush of reverence spread from person to person as the news of her passing on was exchanged. The family came to collect her things and to tell her husband, who was also a patient of ours, and with whom we were dearly close.

Staff members had also been close to the family for a long time. The family confided in us that, because of Melody's husband's overwhelming medical needs, they could not take "Dad" to the funeral. Their plight was met with acceptance and words of caring and comforting. Indeed, no one would judge them.

We offered what turned out to be a good alternative. We con-ducted a closure service. Melody's body was wheeled down to the chapel. Staff, other residents, and family gathered. "Dad" was wheeled in also. We gave thanks for the life Melody shared with us every day. We prayed that the family would be sup-ported as each grieved the loss of a great lady. We told some pretty funny stories about the way Melody joked with all of us. We also shared how much we admired her. We were happy we could be together like this. We were pleased we could provide a dignified time and place for Melody's husband to say good-bye and hear condolences from staff and other residents and friends. Ends like this do not happen without pulling a lot of heartstrings, but we were glad we could tie together a service like this one.

His Spirit Was Great

Matthew could no longer speak in sentences. Instead he repeated the same echolalic phrase over and over. The Certified Nursing Assistants (CNAs) knew him very well. From the inflection of his voice, CNAs knew what this man wanted.

Matthew's room was full of family and staff as we gathered around at his death for a bedside closure service.

One CNA cried as she told how, at first, when she met Matthew he would join her in playing charades until she, after many, many, weeks, finally understood what a change in intensity of the phrase he repeated meant. Another CNA thanked the family for a man who, although he could not clearly express his thoughts, taught her that she would want to make a career of helping people who cannot communicate by everyday means.

We all cried at this bedside closure service. We all miss Matthew. His body and mind were broken long before his death. But his spirit was great. And it touched us deeply and brought meaning to our work and lives.

The Message

Sometimes family cannot be present when a loved one is dying or dies. I received a phone call from the son of a man who was dying. He asked me if he should come right away to his father's side or wait and come to the funeral to support his mother and sisters. The son said he could not afford to come both times.

I could not predict for the young man when his father would die; death appeared to be days to weeks at the most ahead. Even if the son would quickly get a plane, he might miss the deathbed scene. The son told me he had already told his dad he loved him. But, by the pauses in our conversation, I could tell he wanted to say more.

Therefore, I suggested he express his thoughts on tape, send it to me and nurses would play the audiotape at his father's bedside. I told the son that although his father could not speak, he probably could hear and understand. Knowledge of death tells us that the dying hear throughout the death event. The son sent the tape.

This son talked candidly to his father during his father's final days. On tape, he reviewed special experiences the two shared. The son pledged to carry the values taught him by his father to his own children. The father's last moments were filled with the voice and message of love of his son.

Families and staff tell me that taped messages from family and bedside closure services are meaningful and dignified. Families say they are touched by the personal tributes and sharing of memories in the ceremony. For some who die this service is more personal than their funeral service. Staff say bedside closure services give them permission to take the needed time to say good-bye.

The person who takes time to comfort people when death occurs is open to what the dying perceive. They understand without judging and focus on the spirit and not the corpse. They can see that:

- No one dies alone.
- Our spirit can step out of and exist outside our body.
- The universe beyond receives people with
  unconditional love.
- Peace and dignity can accompany death.

I hope that scenes in the stories in this book give you ideas to think about and plan your death event. I hope that you share this book with those you love so you can talk together. You can fashion your final entrance. That's what you can do.

V. Postscript

When you were born you cried
and the whole world rejoiced.
Live such a life that when you die
the whole world cries and you rejoice.
—AMERICAN INDIAN PROVERB

I haven't discovered anything new. I trust I've shed some light on some things that were unknown to you before. I hope these words have been comforting.

Every day I feel fortunate to be with people who share what is happening in their lives. This connectedness is, to me, the heart of being human. I have learned to listen to people. It is clear to me that there always can be more than one true view of the same situation. People see from different vantage points. And the dying see what we living cannot: what life beyond life is all about.

My hope is that your passing on may be balanced between the wonders of science and your needs as a human spirit. When you were born you cried. May you approach your final entrance with joy and peace.

I know you want me to stay
but I can't
Let me go.

You may not understand my choice
but I do.
Let me go.

Where I am at is
a place only
I can see.

If I could
I might show you
what's calling me.

I'm joyful
in awe of the wonderment.
I'm going.

I know you want me to stay
but I can't.
Let me go.

VI. Notes

3. Nightingale, F. (1860). *Notes on Nursing.* New York: D. Appleton and Company, p. 113.

7. Einstein, A. (1930). What I Believe. *Forum,* October 30.

9. Fremit, M. (1989). Near-death experiences: A new understanding. *Physician Assistant, 8,* p. 43.

10. Kubler-Ross, E. (1991). *On Life After Death.* Berkeley, California: Celestial Arts, p. 28.

14. Greyson, B. (1986). Incidence of near-death experiences following attempted suicide. *Suicide and Life Threatening Behavior, 16,* (1), p. 40.

15. Greyson, B. and Bush, N. (1992). Distressing near-death experiences. *Psychiatry, 55,* 95-110.

17. Gunther, J. (1949). *Death Be Not Proud.* New York: Pyramid, p. 192.

24. Monroe, R. (1971). *Journeys Out of the Body.* New York: Doubleday.

24. Monroe, R. (1994). *Ultimate Journey.* New York: Doubleday.

25. Kubler-Ross (1991). *On Life After Death.* Berkeley, California: Celestial Arts, p. 49.

83. Greyson, B. (1986) Incidence of near-death experiences following attempted suicide. *Suicide and Life-Threatening Behavior, 18,* (1), 40-45.

120. Duthie, E. & Tresch, D. (1993). Use of CPR in the nursing home. *Nursing Home Medicine, 1,* (4), 6-10.

VII. Selected Bibliography

Bates, B. & Stanley, A. (1985). The epidemiology and differential diagnosis of near-death experiences. *American Journal of Orthopsychiatry. 55,* (4),542-549.

Duthie, E. and Tresch, D. (1993). Use of CPR in the nursing home. *Nursing Home Medicine, 1* (4), 6-10.

Einstein, A. (1930). What I believe. *Forum,* October 30.

Frankl, V. (1959). *Man's Search for Meaning.* New York: Washington Square Press.

Frankl, V. (1969). *The Will to Meaning.* New York: Penguin.

Frankl, V. (1993). *The Doctor and the Soul.* New York: Vintage Books.

Fremit, M. (1989). Near-death experiences: A new understanding. *Physician Assistant, 8,* 42-50.

Greyson, B. & Stevenson, I. (1980). The phenomenology of near-death experiences. *American Journal of Psychiatry, 137* (10), 1193-1196.

Greyson, B. (1983). The near-death experience scale: Construction, reliability, and validity. *Journal of Nervous and Mental Disease, 171,* (6), 369-375.

Greyson, B. (1983). The psychodynamics of near-death experiences. *Journal of Nervous and Mental Disease, 171,* (6), 376-381.

Greyson, B. (1986). Incidence of near-death experiences following attempted suicide. *Suicide and Life-Threatening Behavior, 16,* (1), 40-45.

Greyson, B. and Bush, N. (1992). Distressing near-death experiences. *Psychiatry, 55,* 95-110.

Gunther, J. (1949). *Death Be Not Proud.* New York: Pyramid.

Kubler-Ross, E. (1991). *On Life After Death.* Berkeley, California: Celestial Arts.

Miller, D. and Grinby, M. (1993). Beyond the utilization of CPR. *Nursing Home Medicine, 1* (4), 13-14.

Monroe, R. (1971). *Journeys Out of The Body.* New York: Doubleday.

Monroe, R. (1994). *Ultimate Journey.* New York: Doubleday.

Morse, M., Conner, D., and Tyler, D. (1985). Near-death experiences in a pediatric population. *American Journal of Diseases of Children, 139,* 595-600.

Morse, M., Castillo, P., Venecia, D., Milsten, J., and Tyler, D. (1986). Childhood near-death experiences. *American Journal of Diseases of Children, 140,* 1110-1114.

Morse, M. & Perry, P. (1990). *Closer to the Light: Learning from the Near-Death Experiences of Children.* New York: Ivy.

Nightingale, F. (1860). *Notes on Nursing.* New York: D. Appleton and Company.

Noyes, R. (1980). Attitude change following near-death experiences. *Psychiatry, 43,* 234-242.

Sabom, M. and Kreutziger. S. (1977). Near-death experiences. *Journal of Florida Medical Association, 64,* (9), 648-650.

Schoenbeck, S. and Hocutt, G. (1991). Near-death experiences in patients undergoing cardiopulmonary resuscitation. *Journal of Near-Death Studies, 9,* (4), 211-218.

Schoenbeck, S. (1993). Exploring the mystery of near-death experiences. *American Journal of Nursing, 93* (5), 42-46.

Schoenbeck, S. (1994). Called to Care: Addressing the spiritual needs of Patients. *Journal of Practical Nursing, XLIV,* (3), 19-23.
Schoenbeck, S. (1994). Long term care nurses face new challenges. *Nursing Matters, 5,* (12), P. 1,6, and 12.

VIII. About The Author

The author, Susan Schoenbeck, is Director of Resident Care for Ingleside Skilled Nursing and Rehabilitation Center in Mount Horeb, Wisconsin. She is a registered nurse, nursing home administrator, and Associate Clinical Professor at the University of Wisconsin–Madison.

An accomplished writer, Schoenbeck's professional work has been published in journals that attract the attention of physicians and nurses from around the globe; she has also written health-care pamphlets directed toward the general public. Schoenbeck served as editor of *Nursing Innovations*, a publication highlighting contemporary accomplishments in nursing. She is the recipient of many honors for her writing achievements.

Schoenbeck is also in great demand as a lecturer on near-death and deathbed experiences and spiritual care. Her audiences vary, from health-care professionals interested in the psychospiritual aspects of life's final stages to community groups gathered primarily to hear stories relating to edge-of-death encounters. She has spoken to many groups and has made television and radio appearances.

In all of her writing and in her speaking engagements, Schoenbeck draws on her many years of clinical nursing, as well as reports from others relating to the edge of death. Her areas of specialty practice are bereavement, counseling the dying and their families, and counseling nursing personnel as they face, in her words, "death as a life event," and seek to provide spiritual care, meaningful interaction with the real person behind the face.

The author is a respected leader in the nursing profession. She is past president of the Madison chapter of Sigma Theta Tau, the international honor society for nurses. Schoenbeck founded the Wisconsin chapter of the International Association for Near-Death Studies, Inc. She has received many awards, including the Universal Voice Award, and, in 1990, was named "Wisconsin Nurse of the Year."

Schoenbeck lives in Madison, Wisconsin, but spends as much leisure time as possible on a pristine section of land in Northern Wisconsin overlooking the Chippewa River. She also retreats yearly to the Benedictine Monastery near Madison.